THE SNAKE

John Crompton

NLB

Nick Lyons Books

Printed in the United States of America

10 9 8 7 6 5 4 3 2 1

Published by arrangement with Doubleday and Co., Inc.

Library of Congress Cataloging-in-Publication Data

Crompton, John, 1893–
  The snake.

  Reprint. Originally published: London: Faber
and Faber, 1963.
  Bibliography: p.
  Includes index.
  1. Snakes. I. Title.
QL666.06C83   1987   597.96   87–3934
ISBN 0–941130–28–2

Contents

INTRODUCTION

The Englishman on the Train

———————◦~~~~~~◦(◦)◦~~~~~~◦———————

Picture yourself boarding the old *Orient Express* in Paris, for a long train journey across the continent to Istanbul. You let yourself into a compartment and find you'll be sharing it with at least one other person, a middle-aged man in rumpled tweeds and a Kitchener mustache. This fellow has the ruddy complexion and rough hands of a yeoman. He sits very straight. For a while, as the train slides west through the Paris suburbs and into the countryside, he keeps properly to himself, occupied with a two-day-old newspaper. From the cut of the tweeds, and from his *Times,* you know he is British. From the martial posture and other clues you guess him for one of those far-flung but loyal Englishmen, the servants of empire, who (in past and simpler ages) spent most of their lives overseas, on military or diplomatic or business assignment, maintaining a level of British civility and equanimity in some very wild places, some very bizarre circumstances. It could be Conrad's Marlow, sitting across from you. But it isn't. As you're about to discover, this man is more in the spirit of Evelyn Waugh. He pulls his nose out of the *Times,* a few words are exchanged, and, before you know how or why, the conversation has turned to snakes.

The man's name is John Crompton, and he has stories to tell.

On another day, another train ride, it might be stories about spiders or bee-keeping or the natural history of ants. Today, though, it is snakes. Istanbul is a long way down the tracks and this garrulous, jovial Englishman seems to be capable of filling that whole distance and time with improbable information about snakes. Set aside your own *International Herald Tribune*. The essence of adventuresome travel is serendipity, and you shouldn't miss this for anything.

Your new acquaintance says: "An American has stated that no snake can travel at more than five miles an hour. That man has much to learn. Probably the fastest as well as the most lethal snake in the world is the Mamba of Africa, and on my patrols in the interior it so happened that I came upon several. . . . When these snakes passed me they seemed to be going at the speed of bolting rabbits—however fast that is. It was firmly believed then that mambas could overtake a galloping horse. That is certainly incorrect, but they did not get such a reputation by travelling at five miles an hour."

He says: "The digestive juices in a snake's stomach are more potent than any in the animal kingdom. This is not surprising when one considers what they have to digest. Without the aid of mastication or the admixture of saliva they have to digest whole creatures, hair, hide, bones and all. The larger snakes who swallow horned antelopes are said to be frequently killed by them, for the horns may pierce through the snake and obtrude outside."

He says: "Snakes are nature's rat and mouse destroyers, but they get little thanks. I once lived in a rat-infested hut in Africa. The creatures even ate the candles. Then a rat snake came along and took up its quarters in the thatch above and the rats disappeared."

Miles go by quickly. Before long it comes out that your travelling companion—who was once a trooper with the Rhodesian Mounted Police, later a shipping inspector in China, still later an air-traffic controller on Iceland—is now an author of nature books. He admits: "From time to time people perfunctorily ask me what, if anything, I am writing about now. When I have said ants or spiders or bees or wasps they have shown a vague polite interest, but when I say snakes they are no longer vague nor polite. A typical comment is, 'Ugh! I shan't read it. I loathe the slimy things.'" Undaunted, he is proceeding with the snake project anyway. He adds: "One woman actually became quite red in the face. She said she could not understand why snakes had been created nor why, having been created, they had been given the power to kill a man in a 'few seconds'. I realized, of course, that she was getting at the Almighty and not me, though when I said a few words for the snake I got the full blast of her wrath, too. The truth of the matter is that it is just waste of breath to say anything in favour of a snake."

But the English travelling man does not let that stop him. He wastes his breath profligately, generously, entertainingly. By the time you both reach the Istanbul station and he disappears in a ramshackle cab, your own brain is abundantly populated—like the state of Texas—with snakes.

Of the six books that John Crompton published between the end of World War II and the early 1960s (all of which are being brought back into print by Nick Lyons Books), *The Snake* might be the most idiosyncratic. Certainly it is not a work of science. (Then again, I know of a respected academic herpetologist in the Southwest, who would say, after a lively and far-ranging seminar: "Well, this wasn't science, but it was fun.") It is less a classic of natural-history writing than a potpourri of garish stories. It does not seem (as does *The Spider,* a gentler and more informative book) the work of a patient amateur naturalist, a man who got down on hands and knees to spend long hours looking his subject in the eyes. *The Snake* is different. There is more distance here between author and subject—possibly because most of Crompton's personal contact with exotic snakes came from his earlier years, before he developed his extraordinary devotion to exactly those types of animal conventionally considered repulsive. That unconventional, endearing devotion is less evident in *The Snake* than in some of the earlier work.

ix

Who knows why. This seems to have been Crompton's last nature book (though I'm not positive, since little is known of him these days), and maybe he was forcing himself to a pattern. Maybe if England itself simply had more native snakes there would be more hands-and-knees flavor to the book.

But even England does have *some* snakes, and even *The Snake* does have some of those characteristic Cromptonian moments of tender, empathetic humor. Of the three English snake species, only the adder is venomous. Crompton writes: "Adders are often kept in captivity though they do not make very good pets. They will eat and can be handled, and when handled do not strike. But they do not like being handled. If caught when elderly, adders are very difficult to tame at all. These, said a writer on the subject, should be let go. I smiled to myself when I thought of the reactions of the neighbors if they knew that someone was releasing elderly adders."

The Englishman on the train, you discover, is possessed of not only an amazing fund of lurid snake stories but also a weakness for elderly adders. My advice is that you sit back and enjoy him. As the expert says: It may not be science, but it's fun.

—DAVID QUAMMEN

1

Upon Thy Belly

*'Upon thy belly shalt thou go and dust
shalt thou eat all the days of thy life.'*

This was part of the serpent's punishment for tempting
Eve in the Garden of Eden, and I remember, as a
small boy, a lady teacher at the Sunday School class I
attended reading us the story from Genesis. A bright boy
then asked, 'What did it go on before?' This flummoxed the
good lady, yet a little elementary knowledge of evolution
would have saved her her embarrassment. The serpent went
on four legs.

When the fishes invaded land they had to make several
radical anatomical alterations. Amongst other things they
had to grow legs, for the better adapted they were to movement in the water the less adapted were they to movement on
land. Amongst the fishy mob of pioneers were the foreparents
of snakes and men, and these, together with the rest, grew
legs. Not very good ones, but they improved as time went on,
and time did go on: many millions of years passed and the
snake still ran about on legs. Then, towards the beginning of
the mammalian era, when the reign of the reptiles was drawing to a close, the snake discarded its legs.

Now the fishes grew legs because they could not move
about on land without them, and it seemed quite impossible

11

that any vertebrate with well-developed ribs and backbone could do so. How did the snake get on? Well, had it held a theory about legless propulsion and set about to prove it, it could not have succeeded better. It would have completely vindicated its theory. Legless, it can travel as fast as a human being, climb trees, travel along the top branches, shooting therefrom like an arrow and resuming its rapid course along the ground, and it can rejoin the element from which it came, its new shape enabling it to swim fast and gracefully.

This mobility was not attained merely by shedding the legs. Other alterations had to take place. All inequalities were smoothed out; neck, shoulders, hindquarters went and the snake emerged as a long, symmetrical cylinder. It seemed to have become all tail, though actually it had shortened its tail, which was now merely a small appendage at the end of an amazingly long body. The body, indeed, seemed ludicrously long but the length was just another of those alterations that had to be made for the snake's new method of locomotion.

In spite of this, even at the present time, the snake has not entirely got rid of its legs. At least, tiny, vestigial remains of what were once hind legs are found inside the bodies of many snakes, while the python has two small external protuberances as leg relics, and carries in its inside the remains of a pelvis.

According to Holy Writ, going upon its belly was a punishment for the snake. Do not believe this, even though it comes from such an eminent source. Probably, as the eras went by and vegetation changed and increased, the snake, with its short legs, found it increasingly difficult to make its way through the herbage. Indeed, it found that twisting, pushing movements got it along better and that half the time its legs were more of an incumbrance than anything else. But what a difference when it emerged as a long, legless cylinder! Now the vegetation that had so hampered it was a help. By thrusting against it with its curving body it could push itself forward, and there were no sticking-out parts to impede it.

Upon Thy Belly

There was another benefit; the undergrowth that now helped its progress hampered that of the prey it pursued.

It is not easy to note how animals move. Watch a dog walking or running, and then say in what order it moves its feet. I doubt if you can—and the dog itself certainly cannot. The same with a snake. The fast ones just flash by in the grass, and all most people can say of the progress of the slower ones is that they 'wriggle'. An earthworm, by bunching itself together and then expanding gets along somehow. A snake cannot do this any more than we can. It has a solid chassis of backbone and ribs, which cannot be squeezed together. Actually it has two methods of movement and the first depends chiefly on the length of its body, which, as stated before, it acquired not as an idiosyncrasy but as a vital necessity. The motion is a sideways waving of the body, starting near the head. The waves travel towards the tail and in doing so press against any vegetation or irregularities in the ground. Each loop, therefore, shoves forward the part of the body that is before it. Though the curves start at the front of the snake, the back curves do most of the pushing, shooting the forepart onward so that it can start the curves again. The tail itself takes no part in the pushing but follows in the direction of the head.

In the past, illustrators used to depict snakes as travelling with their loops in a perpendicular position. They do so now, but mostly in boys' adventure stories. It makes them easier to see, of course, but no snake could move far, if at all, like that. It would also advertise its presence, which is the last thing it wishes to do. Sea serpents are also depicted with their arches showing above the water in a series of loops. There are many sea serpents but all travel through the water with horizontal sweeps.

The second method of progression is quite different. It is an action vaguely similar to that of a caterpillar truck. Under the belly of the snake are large, wide scales, usually called ventral shields. Like slates on a roof, they are attached to the skin at

13

one end only, the end nearest the head. These shields are lifted by the rib above (a snake has up to 300 ribs), moved forward, set down, then pushed backward. The loose hinder end of the shield catches on any irregularity in the ground, and gets a purchase, so that the body in front is thrust on. Again, these movements start near the head and travel down the body as the ribs move in turn. The snake can thus proceed in a perfectly straight line.

That, at least, is how the movement appears, and on account of it many observers have stated that a snake has movable ribs. Actually, the ribs, being attached to the backbone, cannot move at all, but underneath each rib is a muscle. It is this muscle that moves the shields.

Often a snake proceeds by a combination of the two methods. It then seems to 'flow' along.

These methods enable a snake to get over most types of terrain but it cannot move over a perfectly smooth surface, such as glass. Nor, normally, can it get along in loose sand. But the snake is nothing if not adaptive, and species living in sandy deserts *have* learned to travel in loose sand. They do so by a complicated sideways twisting and leaping progress that must be most exhausting.

How fast can a snake travel? It is impossible to say. It might seem that snakes could be captured and tested along a measured distance. But something happens to a snake after it has been caught, something goes out of it. Released, it does not dash away, it merely tries to find cover. Only when disturbed in the wild state, and making for some known retreat, does the snake show its true paces; and neither recorders with stop watches nor measured distances are then available. An American has stated that no snake can travel at more than five miles an hour. That man has much to learn. Probably the fastest as well as the most lethal snake in the world is the Mamba of Africa, and on my patrols in the interior it so happened that I came upon several. When you disturb a mamba it makes at full speed for home (and if you happen to

14

be between it and its hole it may give you a sidelong bite in passing). When these snakes passed me they seemed to be going at the speed of bolting rabbits—however fast that is. It was firmly believed then that mambas could overtake a galloping horse. That is certainly incorrect, but they did not get such a reputation by travelling at five miles an hour.

I remember, too, walking by a lake and disturbing a water snake about eight yards from the bank. It passed me like something from a catapult and reaching the bank shot into the air for several feet before hitting the water and continuing its journey with the wash and wake of a small speed-boat.

A man once raced a snake. It was a small rat snake, not by any means one of the fast species. He was a naturalist and he flushed this snake in India. He knew exactly which hole it was going to make for, and ran full-belt to try and stop it. The distance was about twenty yards and he won by a neck, arriving just in time to cut off the snake's retreat. The snake did not pause but shot up from the ground and sank its teeth into the naturalist's cheek, thus showing not only how fast it could move but how high it could jump.

The loss of a member in evolution is generally called a degenerate or 'recessive' step, yet most of the improvements of the snake came about by discarding possessions. In its legged state it possessed eyelids which moved up and down like those of most of the higher vertebrates. It discarded these at the same time it discarded its legs, and acquired the fixed, unblinking stare for which it is notorious. Eyelids lubricate and protect the eyes, but for a snake, going on its belly through thick, often thorny vegetation, or down small holes, in search of prey this protection was insufficient. It also obscured the vision. So a transparent disc was substituted for the eyelid, a kind of watchglass. In other words, the snake put on spectacles, or rather goggles.

These discs are set neatly in the skin and are, in fact, transparent scales which give full protection to the eyes without

15

obscuring the vision. The eyes behind are still lubricated and emit water which is drained into a gland where it is used for other purposes. Gradually, however, the discs get scratched and vision becomes impaired, but the snake changes its skin several times a year, and with each skin change it gets a new pair of spectacles.

In the beginning, one of the great deficiences of snakes, as with us nowadays, lay in their teeth. These were needle-like affairs, curved inwards. Unlike ours, they could be renewed indefinitely but they still remained small and fragile, capable only of holding prey and of no use for killing or chewing it up. The prey must be swallowed whole and, generally, alive. Other alterations were necessary here; distendable jaws and an arrangement by which the snake could swallow food bigger in girth than itself without choking. That will be touched on later. At the moment we have the snake converted from a legged to a legless animal, nicely adapted to catching prey and capable in one act of swallowing enough food to last it for a week or more. It was also a harmless, almost a necessary creature, hurting no one except, in the main, rats, mice and frogs.

But already evolution was at work prompting (and now it is Evolution that is the Serpent in the Garden) certain snakes to do something about their teeth. There were occasions when big prey was too strong to be held in the proper position for swallowing. What about injecting something into them which would slow down their efforts to fight and escape? So certain snakes, though only a few, became the proud possessors of grooved teeth. These were a pair of teeth on the upper jaw, set well back and having a channel along the outside edge. Along this channel ran saliva from the salivary gland possessing toxic properties that numbed or even killed the small creatures on which these snakes fed.

This was a great help and noteworthy in that the snake had now (as man did later) harnessed chemistry to improve its standard of living. But the snake, though it did not know it, was laying up trouble for itself, as well as for others.

Man, of course, was not present at the time, but if he had been he would have had no cause to dislike these grooved teeth snakes any more than other snakes. Their salivary fluid would only have been very slightly toxic to him, and the grooved teeth were set so far back in the mouth that they would not come into play in an ordinary quick bite such as a snake gives a man.

So there now existed non-poisonous snakes and a few slightly poisonous snakes, but soon Evolution came into the Garden again and tempted the poisonous ones and made some dreadful suggestions to them. Some of them listened, and in due course closed up the groove and formed a tubular fang capable of ejecting a liquid at pressure after the manner of a hypodermic syringe. Further, they lengthened these needle-sharp fangs and switched them from the back to the front so that they would be the first teeth to come into operation in any bite. Further still, they connected these teeth, via a duct, to a venom gland in the head (a reconstructed salivary gland) that supplied the most virulent poison ever known, the ingredients of which are still a secret. So potent is this poison that that made by certain snakes, if injected direct into a vein, will kill a man in less than a minute.

And that is the stage snakes have reached now in their evolutionary career; the majority are non-poisonous, others are back-fanged and poisonous only to small creatures, the remainder are tubular fanged in front and of these a small proportion are deadly dangerous. Whether further changes will come about we do not know. Some scientists think that the evolution of snakes is still in its early stages. In any case they have done very well, they have kept abreast with conditions and improved their standard of living. What they have to fear now is not a cul-de-sac, but man. Man is increasing everywhere and when the rural districts are crammed with houses and small fields, snakes will be brought to bay by their bitterest enemy and annihilated, innocent and guilty alike.

I have not quite finished with anatomy yet, one or two points must be mentioned. For instance, when a creature like a lizard is rolled, as it were, into a long cylinder, something is going to happen to its inside. A lot happened to the snake's inside. Its lungs became compressed into two long, narrow strips; in fact into one long strip, for most snakes lost their left lung. A man with one lung is generally regarded as an invalid and advised not to do too much strenuous work. The snake is in an even worse position, for a drawn-out lung does not function as well as a normal lung. A mammal has its lungs spread out in the chest, close to the air supply. Only one end of a snake's lung is near the air supply. Indeed, the hind end can hardly function as a lung at all, being merely a sort of storage place for air. So although a snake can move quickly enough it is incapable of prolonged exertion. It is a sprinter, not a long-distance runner.

The viscera were greatly elongated and put out of position, those on the right being in front of those on the left, and for some reason, doubtless to do with the rolling-out process, larger. Windpipe, gullet and the rest were all lengthened. In fact a snake's gullet is about one-third the length of the whole alimentary canal, which itself, of course, is very long.

Whilst on the subject of the alimentary canal let us see what happens to the prey a snake catches. The girth of the prey may well be three times that of the snake itself, and since it has to be swallowed whole obvious difficulties present themselves. For one thing, how can it be got into the throat at all? It is only possible because the snake's jaws are not hinged like ours at the base but connected by a sort of elastic ligament which can stretch almost indefinitely. But once the object is in the throat why does the snake not choke? We ourselves would suffocate if we tried to swallow a small apple, let alone something the size of a football. The reason

18

is that the glottis in front of the windpipe (with human beings the glottis is a chamber which, amongst other things, serves to modulate the voice) can, in the case of a snake, be extended beyond the mouth, enabling it to breathe when its throat is blocked.

In due course the prey arrives in the gullet. If the snake is non-poisonous it will probably be alive. Nothing happens to it here. Indeed, apart from mental anxiety, it is as snug as if it were in its own hole. (A naturalist records how a lizard swallowed by a snake remained in the gullet for 24 hours, after which it was ejected none the worse, as the cliché goes, for its experience.) The stomach is next door to the gullet, and sooner or later the prey will be drawn in. The gullet contains no digestive juices, but the stomach does. It is a sort of concentrated acid bath and the unfortunate prey going in head last often has its hindquarters corroded away before the other half is treated.

After the stomach come the elongated intestines leading to the vent. After the vent is the tail, which is distinguished by having small scales instead of large shields on the underside.

Everyone must have noticed the tongue, that slender two-pronged fork that flickers in and out of a snake's mouth for no apparent reason. At the reptile house of a zoo I once heard a man say to his lady friend, 'See its fangs? That shows it's poisonous.' By 'fangs' he was obviously referring to the tongue, and he was maligning a very harmless species.

The tongue has a special sheath inside the mouth into which it is withdrawn when the snake bites. There is also a special gap in the lip through which the tongue can move to and fro, which is why we see the tongue operating through the closed mouth of a snake. The tongue needs this sheath and every protection, for it is an extremely sensitive organ. A snake has the ordinary olfactory organs, but it depends more on its tongue for delicate work. The tongue is covered with sensory corpuscles which pick up the slightest traces of

19

odours. These are, so to speak, collected. Then the tongue goes in and transfers these impressions to the palate which, in its turn, transfers them through its ducts to a remarkable organ called Jacobson's organ which lies above the palate. Incidentally it is this organ into which any tears from the eyes are drawn, and its complexities are by no means fully known as yet. All this complicated process of acquiring knowledge takes place in that fleeting instant between a snake withdrawing its tongue and flicking it out again.

Lizards possess ears with external openings, ear drums, middle ears, Eustachian tubes, inner ears and the rest of the bones, cavities and nerves that convey to the brain the impressions given by vibrating air. Snakes have no ear openings and have lost most of the intricate apparatus that enables human beings to hear speech, appreciate music and, often enough, suffer agony from the general din and clamour of this modern age. Snakes, then, ought not to be able to perceive air vibrations. And this is probably so; experiments have shown that bugles blown loudly and tin cans rattled above them leave them unperturbed. So they cannot be charmed by music. Snake charmers realize this and that is why they move their pipes about while they play. It is the movement that hypnotizes the snake, not the sound.

And yet snakes hear. Everyone knows that sound is conveyed more strongly by solid substances than by air. A train, inaudible otherwise, can be heard approaching from a distance by putting one's ear to the rail. And who has not seen in Wild West films Indians placing their ears to the ground to detect the sound of galloping hoofs? The snake, as we suppose, cannot hear air-borne sounds, but with its lower jaw on the ground it is in a good position to pick up earth-borne sounds. A bone, the quadrate, is connected with the lower jaw and its upper part is attached to a rod-like bone, the columella auris. This bone passes to the internal ear and, since bone is an excellent conductor of sound, the snake hears earth vibrations better than we do ourselves. Even when blindfolded with adhesive tape it reacts immediately to a footstep or the moving of a chair.

This is all very well for snakes on the ground, but what about tree snakes? These often hang from boughs or lie along them. Do they hear? Probably they hear very little and that is why several of them are so dangerous. The mamba frequently hangs over a path and is apt to attack a passer-by. The spitting snake does the same thing. So the general belief is that these snakes deliberately lie in wait for unwary travellers. This is wrong. It is the snake that is taken unawares.

2

Enmity

'*And I will put enmity between thee and the woman and between thy seed and her seed.*'

Aweek ago a man who occasionally does odd jobs rushed up to the house and hammered on the door shouting: 'Get your gun, get your gun!' Thinking, if it was not worse, that a fox was at the chickens I got the gun and asked him what it was. 'A snake! Come quick!' I put the gun back and he led me to a straw rick where a lovely olive and gold grass snake was sunning itself. 'If you'd brought your gun,' he said indignantly, 'we'd have got it. I'll go and get a pitchfork.' I detained him and told him that the snake was as harmless as a canary and explained that its object in being in that rick was to get mice, and added that I wished there were a couple of dozen more of them.

He gave me and the snake a sidelong look and went off without a word, as did the snake into the interior of the rick. Probably I am now regarded as an enemy of society who allows snakes to be at large to the danger of his fellow men.

A snake is the most useful thing that can be on a farm, yet I have never known a farm labourer who would hesitate to kill one and brag about it afterwards over his pint at the local.

22

Enmity

And not only farm labourers: I know a colonel who killed one and showed it to me. It turned out to be not a snake at all but a slow-worm—a great eater of slugs, and the colonel was a keen gardener! But he was unrepentant. 'Always killed them in India,' he said, 'whenever we came across them. Dangerous things, snakes. Don't like them.'

Snakes are nature's rat and mouse destroyers, but they get little thanks. I once lived in a rat-infested hut in Africa. The creatures even ate the candles. Then a rat snake came along and took up its quarters in the thatch above and the rats disappeared. Unfortunately a visitor also came along when I was away on a patrol and spent the night in my hut. When I got back I found a note saying he had found a snake in the hut and shot it. He wrote as if he had saved my life. When I met him later I found it impossible to make him believe that I did not want that snake shot.

The rat and mouse armies of occupation are increasing in every country. Scientists have laboured on the problem but all their efforts have only resulted in a steady increase of these pests. In our country, serious-looking men called Rodent Officers visit overridden premises, look wise and take steps which cause some despondency and loss amongst the rat/ mouse population. But rats and mice breed at a rate that puts even rabbits to shame and the efforts of these officers are like half emptying a bath and leaving the tap still running. Natural enemies, owls, weasels, stoats, foxes account for a few but there are not enough of them nowadays to make much difference (do not smile at the thought of the fox as a mouse destroyer, even the lordly lion in Africa, capable of pulling down and breaking the neck of an ox, will, in times of want, try to catch mice in the grass like any pussy-cat).

Which brings us to cats. Many pin their faith on cats, and cats do kill mice but, lumping them all together, I am not so sure about rats. I will explain why in a minute. What I wish to point out now is that cats cannot go down mouse and rat holes and eat the babies. Snakes can and do. They go down to the nests and swallow every one of the newly born young. This we know from examination of their insides. Frequently whole litters of mice and rats are found. This is what counts in pest destruction.

I shall bring storms of abuse on my head when I suggest that cats as a whole are not the rat destroyers they are made out to be. I do so, however, only from personal experience, and other people's cats may be different from mine. I have had kitten after kitten from guaranteed ratting mothers, only to find when they grew up that they had apparently joined some society for the preservation of rats. Through the barn window I actually saw one of these, with her kittens, waiting until the rats had finished before they went up to their food.

One exception was not a farm cat like the others but a seven-year-old fluffy piece of indolence called Tammy, that spent its life on a cushion in a town flat and did not even know what a rat looked like, though it knew all about larders. Its owners went abroad and I had to take this cat. It changed its ways and went outside a lot. One night I returned and heard a loud squealing near the barn. The squealing stopped and then was renewed farther on in the long grass. This went on at intervals. I followed with a torch and finally came upon the body of a large, newly killed rat. Tammy had disappeared after the running battle was over. After this, ratting became the passion of his life and he became battle-scarred and not so nice-looking.

The history of this once pampered pet is interesting and I am tempted to go on with it a little. He never touched birds, and rarely mice. He was a big-game hunter. I only realized that he was going in for larger prey one afternoon when I was wheeling a barrow backwards and forwards to get turf. Passing the outside lavatory I saw Tammy coming out in a slow, bored way. On my next journey the Corgi dog mouched out from the same place. This was quite usual, cat and dog were accustomed to roam idly about from place to place. But after about

Enmity

fifteen trips I called to mind that every time I had passed that lavatory either the cat or the dog had come out. I went in, and found a partly eaten nearly full-grown rabbit. The two had been spending the afternoon going in and having snacks and putting on their act of casualness for my benefit when I passed. Neither of them licked their lips when my eyes were on them, they were too cute for that. In fact, the nonchalance was rather overdone; it was like that of a man who has bought a bottle of whisky out of licensing hours and passes a policeman just outside the wineshop door.

I closed that snack bar and a week later another was opened in the potting shed. This time their air of detachment got them nowhere and the contents were confiscated.

Another exception was not a cat of mine but a mangy, ginger male that lived in an R.A.F. camp in Iceland. For some reason the rats at that camp (and possibly in Iceland generally) were out-size. Perhaps some mutant gene had cropped up or the mess refuse was particularly nourishing— I don't know, but Ginger killed a lot of them. He caused a panic one afternoon in the officers' mess. We were having tea when Ginger, crooning wickedly, sprang through an open window carrying an enormous rat that was far from dead. It struggled and squealed as he took it to the fireplace, where most of the officers had been standing. 'Had been' is the correct phrase, for I never saw a room cleared more quickly. Bomber and Fighter Command almost fought in the doorway to get out. Heroes of the Battle of Britain pushed and shoved at bomber pilots of equal renown, and the room was left to Ginger and the rat.

Another advantage of snakes as rodent officers is that they swallow their prey. They do not leave it lying about to go bad. I once had a terrible smell in the back bedroom. I never thought of a rat but spent money on professional drain examination. Then I discovered a dead rat under some loose boards in an adjoining outhouse, hidden there by Tammy the

25

Enmity

cat. By some freak of air current the smell had been carried only to that particular bedroom.

Nor do snakes bring in rats alive. A cat belonging to my nearest neighbour used to do this, and one morning his wife had to cook the breakfast with the cat and a rat playing hide-and-seek in the kitchen. For that remarkable woman went on cooking with the rat running about all over the place and occasionally between her feet. Me, I would have dropped the frying-pan and fled! Things have changed. Women seem to have lost their fear of rats and mice since skirts became short. The pictures of women standing on chairs are anachronisms now. I remember a tea party at another R.A.F. mess, this one in Yorkshire, where the steward, for some distorted reason, had tamed the mice in the place by laying down food on the carpet every day at five o'clock, and at five o'clock the mice would come out and run about unafraid. They did so on this occasion, and played around the chairs of the officers and their wives. I noticed strained looks on the faces of several of the men, but the women were unperturbed and some even tried to entice the mice by holding out bits of food. For my part I managed to restrain the urge I had to stand on my chair. In the R.A.F. one had to be brave.

Perhaps I am being unjust to cats, so in fairness I must put on record that I have another one now, a recent acquisition, who *does* catch rats and large ones too. She generally brings them in from outside and lays them at the door, as much as to say, 'Who says cats can't catch rats?' Yet she is a most timid cat and when we got a tiny King Charles spaniel pup would not come near the house for a fortnight.

Man's fear and dislike of snakes is only equalled by the fear and dislike of snakes for man. It is the fear that makes some of them dangerous, for when a man gets close to them and they can see no avenue for escape they consider themselves in deadly danger and may bite in sheer desperation. It is an unnatural thing for them to do, for they possess poison to

Enmity

anaesthetize small prey, not to kill men. However, they *can* deliberately be roused to fury and then their sole ambition is to get a bite in whatever the consequences. This mood is deliberately induced by collectors of snake poisons for anti-venine purposes. Held by the throat, the snake is made to strike at a piece of rubber covering a tumbler. The upper fangs go through the rubber and the poison squirts into the container.

Man is not the only animal to have a fear of snakes. Monkeys are petrified by them, and ungulates dislike them. In China I saw a herd of domestic buffaloes suddenly cease their quiet grazing and begin to run about, stamping on the ground. My interpreter said a snake had got amongst them and they were trying to kill it. I did not find out for I did not investigate. I had had awkward moments with these animals before. The picture of sluggish docility and controlled as a rule by a child of about five, domestic buffaloes seem as harmless as pet lambs. And so they are until a European comes along. They hate the smell of a European and become dangerous when one is near them. An annoyed buffalo, tame or wild, is about as nasty a proposition as there is. I had been warned about this but, as I say, had more than once got into trouble when wandering about by myself. On one occasion I suffered the ignominy of being rescued by a naked Chinese urchin, though at the time he seemed more like an angel than an urchin.

From time to time people perfunctorily ask me what, if anything, I am writing about now. When I have said ants or spiders or bees or wasps they have shown a vague polite interest, but when I say snakes they are no longer vague nor polite. A typical comment is, 'Ugh! I shan't read it. I loathe the slimy things.' (Incidentally, a snake is never slimy; it is as dry as a piece of planed oak.) One woman actually became quite red in the face. She said she could not understand why snakes had been created nor why, having been created, they had been given the power to kill a man in a 'few seconds'. I

27

realized, of course, that she was getting at the Almighty and not me, though when I said a few words for the snake I got the full blast of her wrath, too. The truth of the matter is that it is just waste of breath to say anything in favour of a snake.

The African kraal natives, at least when I lived in that country, are keen observers and have a profound natural history lore, knowing not only the habits of game but those of birds and insects. But they know nothing about snakes. The same fear and hatred that obsesses men throughout the world obsesses them. To them all snakes are poisonous, and to be treated as such, though they *can* distinguish vipers from the others. It has been suggested that in view of the usefulness of snakes the people of countries where they abound should be taught to distinguish them, so as to preserve the harmless species. This is an excellent idea, but not, I am afraid, practicable. The number of species is very large and an un-interested native could not be expected to study and memorize them all. Also their patterns are not constant. Big differences occur in members of the same species. Even the common grass snake is sometimes green, sometimes gold, sometimes grey. The only certain way of identification is an examination of the complicated setting and size of the scales, not easy to make with a snake suddenly encountered!

Snakes, apparently, have other uses than destroying pests. They save murderers from the gallows. The annual number of deaths from snake bites in India is fantastic (though in Africa it is very small) and, before the war, a retired India civil servant told me he was convinced that half these deaths were just plain murder. All a murderer in a remote district had to do was to say the victim died from the bite of a snake, and get his friends (if need be) to back him up. After that the death was merely a matter of statistics.

There is an exception to the universal enmity between men and snakes. A sect in India have made the snake a god and under no circumstances will harm one. The ancient Egyptians deified the cat, presumably because it helped to preserve their corn by keeping down mice and rats. And the Chinese almost deify the frog. They call it the Protector of the Rice because it eats the insect pests that are always liable to attack the plant. Perhaps snake worship springs from the same sense of gratitude.

3

The Bill of Fare

Almost anything it can overpower and swallow whole constitutes the food of a snake. This is where the advantage of poison comes in. A rat, for instance, is liable to fight back when seized by a non-poisonous snake. Usually it is overcome by the snake squeezing it into semi-insensibility, but it often happens that a snake cannot deal with a strong specimen or gets wounded by the chisel-like teeth and has to let go. Let us see a poisonous snake deal with a rat. The rat will be going about its nefarious business and will not see the snake, that master of stealth, getting nearer. At the right distance the head of the snake shoots forward and its fangs bury themselves in the body. It is a movement so quick that the eye cannot follow it. The fangs are withdrawn and the rat, after one squeal, dashes off, no doubt thinking itself lucky to have got away. But after half a minute or so its progress begins to flag. It is panting, its heart is thumping and its legs are numbing. It sinks down to rest.

Meanwhile the snake appears to have forgotten the whole incident. It stays around and opens and shuts its mouth several times as it carefully places the two poison fangs back into their sheaths. Then, its tongue flickering in and out, it glides forwards on the trail. It finds the rat dead, or nearly so, gets it into a suitable position and swallows it at leisure.

Though the Rat snake, the House snake and the Mole

30

snake live entirely on rats and mice when it is possible, with many snakes frogs and lizards are the favourite food. The frog is one of the most unfortunate creatures that exists. It gets a raw deal all round. It is a favourite subject for dissection and vivisection, its legs are jerked from it when alive to provide food for human gourmets, it is a stand-by dish for a host of carnivorae, and one of the chief foods of snakes, who generally give it a very uncomfortable end. No wonder it is becoming rare. In the old days I remember one could kick up several frogs in almost any field, but I have not seen one now for a long time. Not long ago even the London Zoo felt the pinch and issued a kind of SOS for frogs to be sent for their snakes. The reward was a free ticket for the zoo. I do not know what response the request got.

As I have said, a snake's gullet is a kind of waiting-room for the chamber of horrors beyond and in it captives are kept until the stomach is ready for them—sometimes for quite a while. The digestive juices in a snake's stomach are more potent than any in the animal kingdom. This is not surprising when one considers what they have to digest. Without the aid of mastication or the admixture of saliva they have to digest whole creatures, hair, hide, bones and all. The larger snakes who swallow horned antelopes are said to be frequently killed by them, for the horns may pierce through the snake and obtrude outside. But the snake is not necessarily killed, for in the stomach, the digestive juices will dissolve the inside horn portions and those outside will fall off, leaving scars that soon heal.

When the stomach begins to draw the prey in, digestion starts on the first portion that enters, the rest being still in the gullet, which often results in a victim being half corroded away while still alive. So sometimes one almost feels inclined to applaud nature for giving poison to snakes. *Their* prey is either dead or anaesthetized when it goes down.

The toad is a tasty morsel for snakes, but in some ways toads are more intelligent than frogs. Before making the strike

31

a snake has to judge the *size* of its prey. It has to gauge it mentally, for although, as we know, a snake can swallow very large objects, there is a limit. So when a small snake approaches a toad and makes its calculations, instead of running away, for which it is poorly adapted, the toad stays put but blows itself up like a small football until it is about three times its normal size. Viewing it, the snake decides it could never get it down and goes away, and the toad heaves a sigh of relief—or of escaping air.

The Brown House Snake of Africa lives on practically nothing but rats. It is non-venomous and got its name because it enters houses in search of rats. We know how rats have little invulnerable retreats into which they bolt when disturbed. These retreats avail them little in the case of the house snake. In an outhouse in Natal a large rat had one such retreat. There was a crevice and beyond that a joist giving just enough room at the top for the rat to squeeze through. Beyond was a small space about the size of a hat-box. Into this the rat would go and relax when any enemies were around. It knew from experience that it was safe. Its experience, however, had been confined to cats, dogs and men, not house snakes, and when one such entered the outhouse the rat saw it and loped into its retreat. It must have been horrified, and no doubt incredulous, when it saw the front part of the snake coming over the joist into its sanctuary. The snake dealt with the rat and proceeded to swallow it. Down into its gullet went the rat.

The snake then decided to leave but, alas, that part of its body that contained the rat was swollen and could not get past the crevice. The snake was stuck.

It was in this position, i.e. with the hinder part of its body protruding from the crevice, that the householder found it. Ninety-nine out of a hundred householders would have seized this wonderful opportunity of taking a snake by surprise, with only the harmless end to deal with, and smash it to pulp. But this particular man happened to be an intelligent man and did not like rats in his place. So he got to work

1. Head of Puff Adder, showing typical arrangement of Viper poison fangs. Paul Popper Ltd.

2. The Anaconda. The largest snake. Paul Popper Ltd.

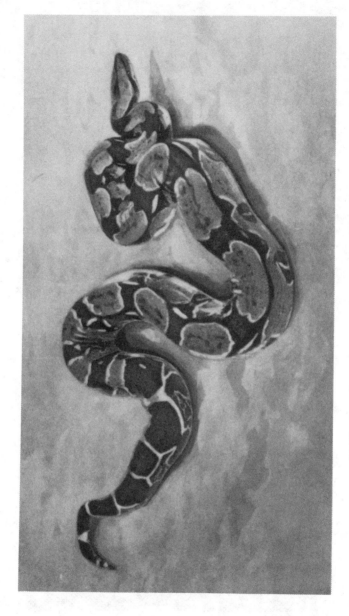

3. *The Boa Constrictor. Feeds chiefly on animals no larger than a rabbit.* Paul Popper Ltd.

The Bill of Fare

prising away stones and wood and freed it and let it go, complete with its rat.

Snake eats snake. Sometimes deliberately and sometimes by mistake. The mistake arises when two of them grab the same prey and commence to swallow it. Soon the heads meet and automatically one head goes down the other's throat and the rest of the body follows. It sometimes happens that a small one swallows a bigger one and half of it protrudes from its mouth for some time, but, assisted by the digestive juices inside, the rest gradually follows.

There is a myth in Africa about a species of snake with two heads, one at each end, and several people claim to have seen it. Investigation has shown that it is one of the burrowing snakes whose hinder end is shaped in the likeness of a head, the vent being very far down and looking rather like a mouth. But there *have* occasionally been double-headed snakes. These, of course, were freaks, like the Siamese twins and other 'monsters'. The Port Elizabeth Snake Park had one. The two heads had two necks, each three inches long, which joined together in the common body, so that whatever one head swallowed went into the common stomach and nourished both of them. The two heads, however, never realized this and if one head caught, say, a frog the other head would try to get it from him. The answer seemed simple—at feeding time always to give two frogs, one to each head. This did not work out as well as expected. At the junction where the necks met traffic from the right head had to be held up until traffic from the left head had gone through, or vice versa. So a mouse or a frog would still be protruding from the mouth of one of the heads after the other head had swallowed its own. The other head would then try to take this food from its mate and a squabble would result. Nevertheless, giving separate food to each was the best plan and on the whole the two heads got on quite well with each other and liked each other's company.

Then, one evening, as usual, two frogs were given, one

apiece, and no further notice taken, but next day it was found that one of the heads had swallowed the other. The swallowed head was carefully abstracted. It was alive, and soon recovered. No harm had been meant by the first head to its friend; it had simply seized the protruding portion of frog, started to swallow it, and the other head had been drawn in. But the swallowed head never forgave the other for the insult. This was one of the back poison fang species, and soon afterwards the aggrieved head struck the other deliberately, bringing its back fangs into play. The poison took effect and promptly killed the snake and both of its two heads. There is an Aesop fable-like quality in this true tale but where exactly the moral comes in I don't know.

Snakes occasionally kill poultry. At an outstation in Rhodesia I was once in charge of a few native police. There was plenty of food—game, bully beef, bacon—and chickens could be bought at the native kraals for threepence each. They were all skin and bone but I have seen not a few recently in poultry shops with the same disqualifications priced at about nine shillings. In spite of all these luxuries I began to crave for eggs, but the natives never had any. They did not eat them themselves and their hens, like the wild things they were, only laid about one batch in a season, and these in some concealed nest away from the kraal. How they got the strength and sustenance to lay eggs at all I do not know. They were never fed by their owners, and for food had to compete with similarly unfed dogs, hosts of wild birds and multitudes of rats and mice.

I decided to rear some real civilized laying hens of modern strains by buying a setting from Bulawayo and putting them under a kaffir hen. The setting arrived and my police combed the kraals until they found a native hen just going broody. I bought her. She settled down on my prepared nest and was soon sitting on six White Leghorn eggs (she was too small to cover any more). In due course she appeared proudly on the parade ground in charge of six baby chicks. Tremendously

34

The Bill of Fare

excited, I went up to examine them and was hit in the chest by a feathered bullet. The mother (called Elsie) had launched herself at me like a modern projectile. She fell, clawing, to the ground and attacked again and I went back where I had come from, leaving her, chattering indignantly, to return to her chicks.

I soon found that it was not really safe to go too near that hen, and before long she turned her attention to the dog and the cat. The fact that the dog was an enormous half-bred Irish wolfhound experienced in bringing down large antelopes and baying leopards made no difference. Elsie decided it must go. It was not safe for her chicks to have creatures like that around. So she made a point of going for both dog and cat whenever she saw them and they, seeing her coming, used to make off. In order to save face they did it in a casual way, rising, yawning, and going away to seek shade—or something.

Elsie's favourite place was the stable. Here she scratched around in the litter, screaming loudly to her chicks when she found bits of grain. It was the duty of the native police to clear that stable out every day and soon, while they worked, they begin to wear harassed expressions and put the job off altogether when Elsie and her chicks were there.

By now I was only in nominal charge of that camp; the real boss was Elsie. Whenever she felt like it she even invaded my office, importantly labelled CHARGE AND ENQUIRY OFFICE. I let her be; to have tried to shoo her out would have meant a scene.

Up to that time I had never seen a snake near the camp, but Elsie found one and (of course) attacked it. It was a non-poisonous species about two feet long and by the time I got to the scene of the disturbance it had been raked and pecked and was practically finished. She killed another snake two weeks later, and may have killed more for all I know.

It was a snake, however, that led to her undoing. One day she attacked a puff adder—and she could not have made a

35

worse choice. I was away at the time, and when I came back the natives showed me Elsie's dead, discoloured, swollen body, and the body of the puff adder, which they had killed with sticks.

By now the chicks were larger than their late mother, but without her indomitable protection they did not last long. Rats, mongooses, wild cats and a host of other creatures carried them off.

Exceptions do occur but, normally, snakes are not inveterate robbers of poultry houses. More chickens are killed by their own inquisitiveness than by deliberate attacks from snakes. They are apt to gather round a snake, watching it with interest and at times giving it an exploratory peck to see what happens. What happens, as often as not, is sudden death. Usually snakes do not like wire-netting but, if the mesh is right, they sometimes squeeze through into poultry runs and kill and swallow a chicken. This may lead to their undoing for, with a chicken inside them, the mesh that admitted them may be too small to let them out. I caught a cobra one morning in this condition in my poultry run and ran to get my gun, elated at having cornered at least one of the many thieves that had been making free with my unfortunate birds. But when I came back a dead, spat-out chicken lay in the enclosure, and the snake had gone. The only one that benefited from this incident was the cat, who had the chicken for supper.

Snakes also eat eggs. An American snake called the Bull Snake was once seen to swallow 14 hen eggs, one after the other, and the only reason it stopped after 14 was that there were no more. The egg goes down unbroken and the digestive juices dissolve the shell. It has been said that some snakes break the egg while it is inside by deliberately exercising internal pressure, but I fail to see how a snake or any other creature *could* exercise internal pressure. A snake has tremendous muscular power when it constricts prey from outside, but that is a different matter. Also, it is very difficult to

36

The Bill of Fare

break an egg by evenly distributed pressure. Try yourself. Take one egg, interlock your fingers and place the egg lengthways between the palms. Now squeeze with all your might. You will not break the egg, unless it is one with an abnormally thin shell.

Even quite small snakes can swallow large eggs. Until one has seen them do it it seems impossible. Really, it is not the size but the smoothness of the egg that makes it difficult, and the rows of incurved teeth on the palate make it more tricky still. With normal prey they help, but not with eggs. On a flat surface a snake cannot swallow an egg; it is like a boy in an obstacle race trying to bite a pendant apple without using his hands. Usually, however, a snake has the nest against which to get a purchase. Once an egg is half-way in the mouth a snake has no further trouble.

It seems to have been proved that snakes can 'smell out' eggs without seeing them. Furthermore, a snake can detect when an egg is addled, and will not touch it. Even slightly tainted eggs are refused. After some recent purchases at the grocers I wish I possessed this sense!

A missionary once got a special sitting of eggs and put them under a hen. One day he heard a commotion and found a snake in the act of swallowing the clutch. He killed the snake and carefully cut it open. He extracted the four eggs that had been taken, and put them back. They hatched with the others. Quite apart from egg or chicken eating, sitting hens attract snakes just by the warmth of their nests.

I am always fascinated by the small kitchen inventions displayed in hardware shops—apple corers, tin openers, grape seeders, fruit juice extractors and scores of other ingenious devices. Nature has invented a similar gadget which is possessed by a snake found in Africa. Apparently it has been patented, for no other snake has copied it. It is an egg extractor and is sited in the gizzard of the Egg Snake (*Dasypeltis scaber*). Attached to the backbone above is a row of small, sharp, enamel teeth fashioned like a saw. Beyond it are some

37

bony protuberances. This is how the contraption works: an egg is swallowed, goes down and is stopped by the protuberances at a spot where the middle of the egg is just under the saw. The saw then works with a to and fro motion and saws through the shell. The contents of the egg flow into the stomach and the shell is ejected through the mouth.

In addition to installing an egg-breaking utensil the egg snake has discarded its teeth. These, as I said, are an obstacle to swallowing eggs. Now only one or two rudimentary relics, which are in the process of being discarded, remain.

This snake must be very fond of eggs to have made these adaptations, but, whilst admiring the ingenuity of the whole set-up, one wonders if it is really necessary—or advantageous. Snakes not possessing the invention can still eat eggs *and* other food as well. The egg snake is debarred from catching rats, mice, frogs and the rest. Incidentally, the egg snake cannot bite and makes a good pet—if you can afford to keep it on fresh eggs.

It has been noted time and time again in snake enclosures, gardens, parks—call them what you will—that a snake, even if hunting, cannot see prey unless the prey moves. It may pass quite close to a rat sitting bolt upright and, providing the rat does not move, will not realize it is there (this does not apply to certain adders, as will be seen later). Even the higher animals are the same. Without the aid of scent, they see only movement. This was brought home to me on a journey I made in Portuguese East Africa. I wished to photograph as much of the animal life as I could and, armed with a heavy reflex camera, performed the usual Red Indian tactics, worming through long grass, dodging behind trees, and the rest. All I ever had to photograph were the rumps of fleeing animals or just clouds of dust. I had to try something else and eventually hit upon the solution which was to stand upright in full view of the quarry, looking at them through the lens of the camera. The animals would stand and stare for long

The Bill of Fare

periods, but provided I did not move they would resume grazing, or whatever they had been doing. They concluded I was a tree stump or some other static part of the scenery. By making one cautious step at a time when no eyes were on me I used to get surprisingly close even to normally very alert creatures. The wind, of course, had to be right.

The yarn that a snake, with its fixed unblinking stare, mesmerizes its prey is a legend that never dies. No prey, confronted with that supposedly deadly gaze, stands rooted and immobile. On the contrary, it is generally galvanized into action. Even rats, though they form one of the snake's chief sources of food, have little respect for any snake that is not 'after' them. Here is the tale of a python. Those enormous but sensitive creatures suffer from shock when captured and go on hunger strike. They have then to be forcibly fed. The feeding consists of ramming bits of rat or other meat down their throats (an operation usually requiring at least three men) and then tying a ligature round the throat, for without it the python would spit the food out. Once, in the Port Elizabeth Snake Park, a rat went boldly up to a python and began to bite into its side. The snake's head came out from its coils and its eyes fixed the rat menacingly. The rat returned the stare and went on gnawing. One bite from the snake would have finished it, but the snake was on hunger strike, so merely jerked it off with its head. The rat came back and resumed feeding. Blow after blow from the snake's head sent the rat spinning, but it always came back. And this went on until the rat had had enough blood and flesh for its present needs and left the snake to continue its hunger strike.

On another occasion a shrew was thrown into a box as food for a small snake. The shrew was about the size of a thimble, so would not last the snake long, but when the cage was opened the next morning to give the snake more food it was found that the shrew had killed the snake and had already eaten quite a bit of it.

Monkeys, however, get hysterical in the presence of snakes.

39

The Bill of Fare

I was trekking in Africa and having a rest under some trees when a mob of monkeys came along above and discovered me. The usual chattering and what sounded like (and probably was) ribald laughter took place. Suddenly the jeers and baiting changed to shrieks and the trees shed monkeys that dropped to the ground like ripe coconuts and dashed off, the mothers dragging their infants by the hand after them. I suspected a leopard, though leopards do not usually prowl about in daylight, but going to the place where the disturbance seemed to have started one of the native carriers spotted a python moving along a branch, and as soon as he pointed it out I saw it too.

Monkeys have every right to be terrified of pythons, but they are equally terrified of small snakes which could not possibly be interested in them. But then monkeys like 'scenes' and welcome any excuse for making one—and they are not, I think, alone in this.

Snakes will drink milk, and there is a widespread belief that they will milk cows by sucking their teats. A Dutch farmer I visited in Rhodesia told me he was badly plagued by one (or maybe more) that milked one or two of his cows practically dry every night. At dawn he used to go round the cattle kraal with his gun, hoping to see the snake making off. When I expressed my doubts he gave an offensive laugh— why, one of his own umfans (small boys that look after the cattle) had actually *seen* a snake milking one of his cows in broad daylight! I thought it best to say no more but umfans themselves are very fond of milk and in this case were obviously making yet another scapegoat of the poor maligned snake. A snake's mouth is full of small teeth and the cow that would submit to being milked by one would have to be chloroformed first.

4

Amity

The idea of a snake as a pet does not appeal to everyone, nor, it may be added, does it appeal to most snakes, so it may come as a surprise to many to learn that, according to Curran and Kauffeld, one of the largest non-poisonous snakes in America, the Indigo Snake (*Drymarchon corais couperi*) has been hunted to the verge of extinction in the demand for snake pets. This beautiful blue creature is docile and amiable and seems to like being made a fuss of. Also (like many snakes) it can never be induced to bite a human being. True, on first being captured it *may* give a slight peck, but after that it never attempts to bite again. This snake is also in demand for 'show business', where snake charmers can show their control over a large and handsome snake which is probably billed as being deadly venomous.

Other snakes make good pets. The British grass snake is one. I have handled these a lot but have not kept them as pets because my wife objects to them in the house. Yet they are cleaner than most dogs and cats and do not shed fur over the chairs and carpets nor jump in and out of open windows with muddy paws nor demand bowls of food every day. My wife thinks they might keep visitors away (no bad thing in certain cases!) and certainly the 'charlady' coming upon a snake when dusting under the sofa (if she went that far) might react unfavourably—and charladies these days are not people to

41

discourage. Those who have kept them, however, tell me that grass snakes never bite, but, during the first week of captivity, if suddenly picked up, may make a lunge at the face or hands as if about to do so. But they do not open their mouths, so that all one gets is a slight blow from their nose. After this pathetic attempt at self-expression they settle down nicely and can distinguish their owners from other people.

This particular snake has one drawback in its very early stages of capture. Owing to fright, it may discharge through its vent a substance with a horrible smell—quite nauseating. The other two British snakes, the smooth snake and the adder, do not do this or, if they do, the discharge is odourless. The smooth snake is rare, the adder is docile and well behaved, but for obvious reasons few people wish to keep adders.

Apparently some grass snakes in captivity continue to make a discharge, but only when frightened, for Gilbert White, in *The Natural History of Selbourne* writes: 'I knew a gentleman who kept a tame grass snake which was in its person as sweet as any animal while in good humour and unalarmed; but as soon as a stranger, or a dog or cat, came in it fell to hissing and filled the room with such nauseous effluvia as rendered it hardly supportable.'

The idea that a venomous snake is a fierce snake is wrong. Once they realize that their human owner is not an enemy, any urge to bite disappears and is reserved for their normal prey. In America rattlesnakes are occasionally kept as pets and the owner becomes very fond of them, and, apparently, they of him. According to Fitzsimons the only poisonous snake in Africa that cannot be tamed is the puff adder. I am not going to argue with this, but I would not like to try taming a Black Mamba. An example of a venomous snake that makes a good pet is the Indian Cobra. It is docility itself.

One certain way of being bitten is to pick up a snake you are afraid of. It is known that fear causes the emanation of a smell that infuriates nearly all animals. Most accidents to wild animal tamers are due to their suddenly feeling fear and

Amity

giving off the deadly scent. It is the absence of this fear smell which explains why young children have often been found playing unscathed with really savage dogs and other creatures. Putting on an act of boldness if there is fear underneath gets one nowhere with the lower animals, they detect nervousness by smell, not actions.

Why do people keep snakes as pets? Exhibitionism undoubtedly in a lot of cases. In these days of drab uniformity it tends to distinguish them from their fellows. I am told that many film actresses have kept a tame snake, and no doubt they took care that their publicity agents made the most of it. But some do like their snakes. I knew a Rhodesian farmer who kept his mostly inside his shirt, whence it would occasionally poke out its head to see what was going on in the outside world. Snake-keeping schoolboys, too, are generally fond of them.

But do tame snakes like their owners? I think so, mostly. They certainly get to know them and show signs of uneasiness when they are away. Some will take food from no one else and will show fear in the presence of strangers—possibly because the strangers are afraid of *them*.

But the snake's liking for its owner and its pleasure in close contact with him is not entirely altruistic. The snake is cold-blooded and has to get its warmth from outside sources. In spring it will search for any patch of sunlight and lie and bask in it, and it finds the warmth of a human body pleasant. In spite of that double-crosser, Eve, snakes prefer women to men: women are warmer and softer.

In Africa a farmer once persuaded me to take over his pet snake while he was away on leave. It was a mole snake, about three feet long, and soon made itself at home in the camp. In fact, I frequently found the cat asleep on my pillow, and the snake asleep underneath the bedclothes. The snake was more attached to the cat than to me, and the only unpleasantness between them was when the snake (its name was Ghoo) once swallowed a small mouse the cat had brought in to play with. The cat bit the snake, which retired into a corner and sulked for the rest of the day.

Ghoo got into the habit of coming into the office while I was there, and lying up somewhere. One morning a farmer arrived. As well as being Trooper l/c Police I was, amongst other things, Acting Cattle Inspector, and this farmer wanted a permit to move some stock. He did not look very well and told me that on the way from his farm he had stayed the night in the shack of a farmer friend and, with the help of a bottle of whisky, they had passed an agreeable evening. Whilst filling in his permit I looked up to ask a question and saw that his face was grey and his bulging eyes were staring at my desk. Ghoo had come out from the letter tray and with her head well over the side of the desk was directing a fixed stare on the intruder. I explained things hastily, and as soon as he was convinced that the snake existed in fact and not merely in fancy, and with the help of a few restoratives, he recovered. But, I am glad to say, he did not spend the night at the camp as he had proposed.

Incidentally, this same farmer was killed, supposedly, by a donkey about three years later. He moved to another area and on his journeys here and there and to Bulawayo had to pass a small wayside hotel that used to be visited at week-ends by folk from Bulawayo. 'Pass' perhaps is the wrong word for he always ended by staying the night. According to a friend who told me this story he spent one evening there solidly drinking dop (Cape brandy). Finally he went unsteadily to his bed. He awoke about three a.m. with (as he himself said later) a mouth that tasted like salted leather and a head that didn't seem his own. There was an orange orchard adjoining the hotel and he felt an urgent desire for oranges. He got up, went out and into the orchard. It was starlight but not moonlight. He went to the nearest tree and was picking an orange when a cavernous mouth appeared from behind the trunk and, shattering the stillness, brayed direct into his ear with the volume of a concentrated jazz band. He knew, he said, no more and 'passed out'. An hour later he crawled back to bed. He stayed at the hotel two more days before he felt fit to go home. A week later he was found dead in his shack, whether of D.T.s or heart failure I do not know, but Sally, the donkey that grazed in the orange orchard of the hotel, undoubtedly hastened his end.

Scattered over the interior of that country, often in the most remote places, are, or used to be, stores, called native stores, kept by Europeans. Except possibly for a native wife, these storekeepers led the loneliest of lives. They must have preferred it that way but they certainly welcomed any white visitors, and their hospitality was overwhelming. They were mines of information about natural history and native lore and it was a privilege to stay with them. These stores were quite large; shelves and shelves crammed with every sort of goods and food round the walls, a long counter, and on the floor sacks of mealies, mealie meal, flour, potatoes and the rest. The ignorant might wonder how, in such isolation, the store got any customers, but distance (and time) is nothing to a native and the store was a rendezvous for all the kraals around, even those fifty miles or so away. They brought in cattle, goats, skins, grain and other things, for which they received money which they spent in the store. A grocer's shop in rural England is the centre of all the gossip in the village, but that is nothing to the gossip that goes on in native stores in Africa.

All this, by the way. I am merely trying to describe what a native store was.

I once had to make a hundred-mile journey by mule in country strange to me, and on the map I saw marked 'native store'. I selected it as a stopping-over place and managed to find my way there. It was the usual sort of place, pole and mud walls and galvanized-iron roof, with the name of the proprietor, W. Osborne, over the door, but what took my attention was another, smaller notice close by: THE SNAKES ARE HARMLESS.

Amity

Later, I asked Osborne about the snakes. He said he had three house snakes that roamed the store and outbuildings. (He found one under the counter and showed it me.) He had, he said, been a storekeeper for years, in other stores as well as this, and had got such an aversion to the hordes of mice that always flourished in a store that he had decided to give it up. If he lifted anything from a shelf, a mouse was sure to scurry away. They gnawed into the sacks and ate and contaminated the contents. They made nests in unexpected places and always there was the sound of mice running about. Cats were no good, there were so many secure hiding places for the mice. Then he thought of snakes and got these snakes sent him by a friend who lived in Port Elizabeth. He kept them shut up in his bedroom for a week so that they could get used to him, and then let them loose in the store. Gradually the mice grew less until now, he said, there were practically none.

The natives could not read the sign but soon came to know that the snakes were harmless; in any case the snakes rarely showed themselves when natives were there. Apart from his mental relief he reckoned he saved £100 a year by the absence of mice.

I have found a lot of keepers of tame snakes a little inconsiderate (I suppose I was myself in the incident related earlier). They enjoy the surprise their pets give to others and are apt to forget that this surprise sometimes amounts to severe shock.

5

A Host of Enemies

To be a successful enemy of snakes calls for knowledge, finesse and training, and the chief item of knowledge is that one bite from a snake is fatal. There must be no blind courage, no rough and tumbles, for it avails little to kill a snake if one dies shortly afterwards. Non-poisonous snakes can, of course, be dealt with in this crude way, but it is doubtful if the hereditary enemies of snakes know which species are poisonous. I have heard it stated that snakes developed poison glands both for killing prey and as a protection against enemies. This is nonsense. Any enemy that attacks a snake and gets bitten is almost certain to kill the snake before it itself succumbs. Hundreds of rash dogs have been killed by snakes but I wager a bet that the snakes died first.

One of the most remarkable things about the poison of the worst snakes is its virulency. About the largest prey they have to kill is a rat. Then why make poison that can kill a man or an elephant whose death is of no use to them? The spider also bites its prey and injects poison of a potency sufficient to kill a sparrow or a mouse but the effect of this poison on man (with the exception at times of the Black Widow and one or two of her relatives) is negligible.

There is a common idea that certain snake-killing animals —pigs, mongooses, badgers, etc.—are immune from snake poison. No animal is immune from snake poison, but some

47

are protected by thick coats of hair, rubbery hides, or layers of fat which prevent the poison from getting into the bloodstream.

Probably because of Kipling's *Rikki-Tikki-Tavi* tale the mongoose is generally regarded as a sort of dedicated Dragon Slayer with regard to snakes. This reputation is deserved, though there are others, including meercats, muishonds, polecats and many others, which are just as formidable, if not more so. The mongoose depends (apart from its knowledge) entirely on its quickness. And it *is* quick. A friend of mine and myself, in Rhodesia, came upon a hole in the ground which we thought might contain a mongoose. My friend suggested catching it. Knowing how a mongoose can bite I was not a very enthusiastic participant in what followed. My friend got his blanket from his horse and laid it on the ground by the hole. Then he cut down a long, thin branch from a tree and trimmed it, leaving a leafy bit at the top. This he thrust into the hole and twisted round. Presumably he thought the mongoose would walk out and surrender. What emerged from that hole was something like a shell from a gun. A misty grey streak shot through the air, alighted farther away, and disappeared. That's a mongoose, that was, we decided, but we had not been able really to see if it were a mongoose or not.

So quick is the mongoose that with most snakes it does not really need to take any precautions at all. One bound lands it just behind the head, and a crushing bite into the neck finishes the snake. With snakes like the cobra, however, different tactics are called for. When on the defensive the head of a cobra and about a third of its body are poised erect. The erect position is like a steep spring that can shoot out with lightning speed. The blow is aimed with such force that after it has been made the snake is flat on the ground. In a split second, however, the cobra is back in its normal defensive position. The mongoose dances about in front of the cobra and encourages it to strike, but its timing is so good

4. The South African Python. Paul Popper Ltd.

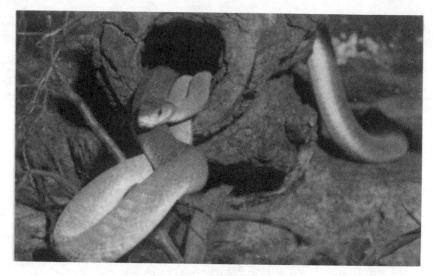

5. *The Black Mamba. The most venomous snake.* Zoological Society of London.

6. *The Common Cobra. Showing 'spectacles' at the back.* Paul Popper Ltd.

that when the strike comes the mongoose is always about an inch away from the snake's head. Snakes, as we know, are not possessed of great stamina. The cobra tires, and as times goes on the raising from the horizontal position to the erect becomes more and more of an effort. The mongoose is waiting for this and at the right time makes a quick dart in, and all is over.

There are certain snakes that defend themselves less conventionally and can strike sideways. Against these the mongoose is not so successful. I know of no fights between a mongoose and a mamba—the mamba does not wait to be attacked—but I should say that the mongoose would have no chance.

I recently read about an island in the Pacific. It was a pleasant place and fertile but it had one drawback; it was infested by snakes. Snakes were everywhere and the natives were almost in a state of terror. They used to implore any sailors in ships that visited them to bring them some mongooses, for they had heard what proficient snake killers these were. One day they actually got their wish, for a ship arrived with a cage full of mongooses brought by some sailors specially for them. The sailors were suitably rewarded and the mongooses let loose. They were a terrific success; the place suited them, they bred, and they lived on snakes. The snakes, in fact, were easy meat for them; all that had to be done was to dart in and bite their necks.

Even with the best possible motives the introduction of new species of fauna and flora into strange places does not always turn out to be as beneficial as might have been expected. Look at rabbits and prickly pears in Australia!

But the islanders were very happy. The scheme had worked well, the snakes were disappearing and at the same time the mongooses were multiplying. There were none of their natural enemies on the island, so there was no check to them. Then the obvious came to pass. With diminishing snakes and increasing mongooses, food for the latter grew scarcer. Soon

A Host of Enemies

it was a common sight to see two mongooses fighting for the possession of one snake, and before very long the snakes were practically exterminated.

The mongooses had to do something about it—and did. The islanders went in for chickens on a pretty large scale. Chicken and eggs were their main standby. Soon these became the main standby of the mongooses also. A mongoose, if it wishes, can get into almost any place. So the last state of these islanders was worse then the first. No doubt they are now trying to import some animal that kills mongooses—and if they do will probably land themselves in another mess.

Many snake v. mongoose fights have been staged in cages —often little more than wooden boxes. This is unfair for the mongoose and valueless as an experiment. The snake protects itself in a corner and the mongoose's essential freedom of movement is hampered by the confinement. If a mongoose is bitten it is very well aware of its fate. After killing the snake it retires to some corner and waits there motionless until the poison has done its work.

The polecat has an unsavoury reputation in Africa. Attacked by a dog or other animal it will squirt the contents of a gland situated in its hindquarters into the face of its foe. I have seen this happen with several dogs and the result is as if the dog had been hit with a shotgun. It rolls about in agony and seems unable to get its breath. This goes on for about three minutes (more than ample time for the polecat to get away) and then the dog becomes its normal self except that it keeps rubbing its face with its paws. But more trouble is in store for it, especially if it has been accustomed to live in the house. It is like one of those unfortunates pictured in advertisements who have no friends owing to B.O. or B.B. The stench from the polecat secretion is the foulest I know, and it lasts for over a week. By now the dog is quite unaware that it reeks to high heaven and cannot understand why no one, including other dogs, will have anything to do with it. As I say, I have seen polecats squirt dogs (sometimes on the body instead of the face) but the usual thing is to have one's dog come home after a solitary walk and enter the house unobtrusively. The air in the house immediately becomes blue and the most fanatical dog lovers will hound their pet out of the place and keep the door shut. Yet the polecat itself is a clean, odourless little animal. It is like a large ferret with broad longitudinal black and white stripes and its thick fur, which is quite sweet smelling, is in good demand. It has never any occasion to use its stink bomb on snakes. It attacks quickly and crushes the neck.

The meercat of Africa is one of the most attractive animals I know. When captured it becomes tame in about a week. It adores petting and will snuggle under one's coat for hours. It has large bright eyes and is a born comedian, playing tricks of its own for hours. It is not a cat at all, and does not look like one. It has a pointed nose and its favourite attitude is sitting bolt upright on its hindquarters with its forepaws dangling in the air, on the look-out for anything that might be of interest—and there is little that goes on that is not of interest to the meercat. It eats almost anything, beetles, worms, rats, mice, and it is amongst the professionals in its dealings with snakes, which its lightning speed enables it to kill almost immediately, though as a rule it avoids the large poisonous ones. Mongooses, polecats and meercats generally eat the head of the snake before any other part, perhaps wishing to get that dangerous member out of the way. But before eating any part of it the meercat goes down the snake's body crushing its backbone at intervals so as to stop any awkward threshing movements.

When two dogs fight, discretion is cast to the wind. They care not how many bites they receive so long as they can inflict more. So a dog would seem to be ruled out as a snake killer; though many have entered the lists. It seems a one-sided contest, as if two boxers entered the ring, one of whom had only to get one blow in to be judged the winner, even if the prize was posthumous. I myself have known no dog snake

A Host of Enemies

killers personally, though I know of many snake dog killers, but I have heard several tales from dog owners. Judging by these there is no doubt that a dog can acquire a technique for coping with snakes. This is not surprising, for the dog is an intelligent animal, but snake-killing is a hazardous career for dogs. They are not born to it. Their ancestors, wolves and (possibly) jackals, always give snakes a wide berth, though otherwise they eat almost anything.

Once the subject was introduced, an acquaintance of mine, retired from India, could never resist talking about his red setter, a famous cobra killer. It attacked the cobra from behind and never failed to kill it. No cobra, he said, had a hope once his dog appeared. I asked him where his dog was now and he said it was dead. I asked him what it had died of, and he said it had died from a cobra bite. It had attacked a cobra but the mate of the cobra was alongside and bit and killed the dog.

I could give many other examples of dog snake killers, including a fox-terrier that used its brains and was quick and was for many years, apparently, a deadly scourge to the snakes in the neighbourhood. One night, however, it returned home with one side of its head badly swollen, and died. With dogs, it is always a matter of the pitcher going to the well once too often.

A dog in Rhodesia when I was there appeared to be an exception. He was a mangy mongrel that always slouched about in a tired way as if he was weary of the world. He had no technique whatever with snakes but killed them by the dozen, being generally bitten in the process. In some miraculous way he must have become immune. He must have received a few small bites, or bites from not very virulent species, at the beginning of his career, and recovered, then gradually built up an almost complete resistance. His master proudly claimed that there was no snake living that could do him any harm. But even this cast-iron pitcher went to the well once too often. He met a snake that *could* do him harm and

A Host of Enemies

he came home badly swollen. What species of snake it was is not known, but the dog died in about twenty-four hours.

The ancestral stock of the domestic cat is rather a mystery. It is improbable that it came from the untameable wild cat, that is now so rare, but if it did it would inherit no special gifts as a snake killer. A farmer I knew used to maintain that any cat can kill a snake. Where he got the idea from I do not know, but he stuck to it. He had a nearly full-grown cat that used to follow him about. One day they encountered a small snake and he watched with interest to see how the cat would deal with it. The cat crouched, staring, then advanced and gave the snake an inquisitive pat on the back with its paw The snake's head flashed round and bit the cat in the leg. It was not a very virulent species but the cat died, a victim not of its own folly but of that of the farmer.

On the other hand, Fitzsimons tells of a cat named Tom who belonged to a Transvaal farmer. Almost every night this cat brought back a snake which it had killed, or not killed, for like all cats it liked its prey to keep moving as long as possible. I am always a bit dubious about these tales people tell of snake-killing dogs and cats unless one knows the species they kill, for the non-poisonous species far outnumber the poisonous. However, in this case the man actually saw his cat meet one of the most deadly of snakes, a puff adder. Like the other farmer, though with more justification, this man had no qualms for his cat. The puff adder is a slow mover when travelling, but it is quick enough on the strike. The farmer watched the combat with interest. Unlike mongooses etc. Tom made considerable use of its claws. This was to be expected, the claws more than the jaws being the natural weapons of the domestic cat. This cat made repeated feints at the snake and then, as the snake began to tire, gave it quick, damaging rakes with its paws. The attacks continued until finally the snake was laid low. This was very creditable, but I am sure the puff adder must have been a small one; no domestic cat could kill a full-grown puff adder with its claws; the hide is too tough, for one thing.

The inevitable, of course, happened. One night, Tom came home with his head swollen and passed out in an hour or so. The truth is, however clever a cat or dog may be there is always some snake who is cleverer, and one day the two will meet.

But of all snake enemies, birds are the greatest. They can spot them more easily from overhead, and their talons and legs are, in a way, armoured. There are some eagles in Africa that seem to hunt snakes in preference to anything else. One is always hearing tales of eagles picking up snakes, soaring aloft with them, then faltering in mid-air and coming crashing down; the cause being a bite, or the snake twining itself round its captor's neck. These must have been very inexperienced eagles, for the majority know quite well how to deal with a snake.

A bird does not need to be an eagle to cope with snakes; it can be one of those slow, meditative creatures. There are many, including storks, but the most talented is that fascinating creature, the secretary bird. A tuft of feathers makes this bird appear to have quill pens tucked over its ears, and its gait reminds one of some tall, elderly, Dickensian clerk in tight trousers. I have met several of them and they move with such sedate dignity that one thinks it will be easy to get close to them, especially since the bird rarely shows any signs of alarm. But the closer one gets the farther one gets, as the Irishman said. Although the bird has not appeared to increase its measured pace in the slightest degree, it has drawn farther away. Once I went after one on a horse. It merely took lazily to the air when I got too close.

When a secretary bird meets a snake it thrusts out its expanded wings on either side. As it approaches, the snake attacks, but it attacks the outspread pinions and is smashed forward with a powerful blow. If the snake is large and aggressive it gets in several bites, but it only bites quills, for

A Host of Enemies

the bird is adroit at judging direction and interposing an outstretched wing, rather like a matador with his red cloth. This continues as long as necessary, then the secretary bird with its long legs and talons rakes the tiring snake to pieces on the ground and eats it with sedate enjoyment.

I was lucky enough to see one of these duels. It was in Portuguese East Africa and I had left my camp to have a look around. On a small hill I took out my glasses and surveyed the country. Not very far away was a secretary bird, pacing along in its usual preoccupied manner. I moved the glasses round the horizon and made out a herd of zebras and a herd of wildebeeste. Nothing very interesting, so I came back to the secretary bird. This thoughtful old gentleman seemed now to be dancing, in a funny way as if full of rheumatism, and his wings were spread out like a turkeycock's. I then made out a snake in front of him, probably a cobra, for part of its body was erect. Presumably the snake struck, for the secretary bird clouted it with its wing and then danced backward. He advanced, and again the snake struck but received such a buffet that it was lifted clean off the ground. The bird was on it immediately and busy with talons and beak, raking the snake and bashing it on the ground. It then ate it, in the usual meditative way, as if wondering if it was as good as the last one it ate, and proceeded on its way to the office—or wherever it had come from.

The whole thing took little time and it occurred to me that if, when I searched the horizon with my glasses I had seen something more interesting than a few antelopes, a lion, for instance, I would have spent some time observing *him*, and when I came back for a second look at the secretary bird I would have found it strolling along exactly as before and would never have dreamed that it had been doing anything else in the meantime. There is a lot of chance in observation.

Turkeys, too, especially in America, are dangerous enemies of snakes. They adopt the spread-out wing method.

55

A Host of Enemies

The most formidable animals in the world, though fast disappearing, are the driver ants of Africa and (of a different type) South America. They spend their lives marching in large armies, sometimes about a million strong. The huge python is a favourite prey, if drivers can be said to have a favourite prey, for they just eat every creature they come across. The python is a slow mover and has no hope if discovered by drivers. His tough, scaly hide is no protection against the pincers of these ravenous butchers. Slow as he is, the python cannot move at all after swallowing a large victim such as an antelope. Before swallowing it, however, the python has to constrict and kill it. It is a common belief that the python then leaves the dead body and makes a circular tour to satisfy himself that there are no driver ants in the vicinity. But what would be the sense of this? If he *did* find any driver ants in the vicinity they would find *him* and destroy him. He might just as well get on with his meal and trust to luck.

The domestic pig is an animal I like. His earthy grunts, his enjoyment of his food and his comical little eyes attract me, and I cannot blame those women who take one about on a lead with a blue or red ribbon round its neck. But pigs are descended from great fighters and can be less endearing than they appear. A sick man, alone in his hut in Rhodesia, was once killed by his own starving pigs, and lambs are by no means safe from them. Nor are snakes. A herd of pigs will clear snakes from a large area in a short time. Any bites they receive are usually delivered into fat tissue and the poison never gets into the blood-stream.

The frog, the chief victim of snakes and of a host of other animals as well, occasionally gets its own back for it will swallow the newly born young of snakes if it comes upon them.

But all snake enemies amount to nothing compared with man. The other enemies preserve the balance of nature, man does not, and is always being mystified and annoyed when

56

the elimination of one supposed pest brings greater trouble from another. He now uses almost every lethal weapon he possesses (and these are many) against snakes, who leave untouched and uncontaminated all his food supplies, while indirectly he protects the rats and mice, who do not.

6

Cold Operations

────────·vv⌒⌒⌒⌒(◉)⌒⌒⌒⌒vv·────────

Before touching on the hibernation of snakes I should like to deal shortly with hibernation in general.

Cold is the enemy of life. On this planet life can only exist between a small margin of temperatures. On the cold side, many animals, polar bears, seals, penguins, husky dogs, Manchurian ponies, can live in what seems very severe cold indeed, but this cold is little more than a mothering warmth compared with the untempered cold of outer space. Man, in his natural state, cannot exist in cold regions. He *does* exist in such regions, but only by wearing furs and wool and wind-proof clothing, by making fires and building huts and houses. Deprived of these he would hardly last one day. True, French prisoners in Dartmoor prison once showed how resistant to cold the unprotected human body can be, but I am talking of colder places than the south of England.

The inhabitants of the cold countries of the north have always been more virile than dwellers in hot countries, but the fact remains that cold is a killer and the northern races have become more virile on that account. Cold has killed off their weaklings and left the strong. They became mentally more active also through the necessity of work and thought, getting and making clothes, food, fires, what time the natives of the tropics lounged with blank minds in the sunshine and ate what grew close by them.

Cold Operations

Our primitive ancestors advanced and retreated as the glaciers of the ice ages retreated and advanced, but what protection against cold they had, we do not know. It is certain, however, that man is now growing less and less able to withstand even moderate cold. The civilized northern once-virile nations are taking more and more to living in centrally over-heated houses and schools. Even with explorers, the rigours endured by, for instance, the members of Scott's last expedition will probably never have to be faced again. Polar expeditions are now mechanized and mothered by planes, while food, that important anti-cold agent, has no longer to be limited by carriage on ponies and dog sledges. Had Scott arrived at the South Pole as it is now—a kind of luxury hotel —he could easily have made the return journey to his long-distant base. The other perils of such a journey—crevices, etc.—of course remain; I am speaking only of cold.

Snakes and reptiles are cold-blooded, so their activity, or non-activity, is regulated by the outside temperature. In cold spells they slow down to an extent that practically amounts to temporary hibernation. And during their real hibernating periods no change in their systems is required. Not so, mammals. With mammals (and birds) nature made one of her very occasional sweeping changes of model. She produced animals that made their own heat, and so were more or less unaffected by the outside cold, especially when they wore fur or feathers to preserve their heat. (Fur would be useless to a snake in winter for it has no inside warmth to retain.) Therefore these new animals were able to keep active in almost any place all the year round. But they had to pay a big price for it. That interior stove of theirs is expensive. Instead of being able to relax like the reptiles, they have to be ever on the move to obtain fuel. Whilst cold-blooded animals can fast, if necessary, for long periods (four years in the case of some of them), the warm-blooded must take in food at frequent intervals (watch any cow or sheep in a field), the bulk of which food is needed not for tissue-making but for stove fuel.

Cold Operations

Nevertheless this model has been a great success, and warm-blooded animals have become completely dominant on earth.

So why did certain mammals discard their advantage? Why did some of them choose to spend the winter in the same way as the reptiles? And how did they manage to do it? For hibernation entails a fast, often six months or more, and I have just said that the mammalian system requires frequent supplies of food.

There is a lot that is still puzzling about the hibernation of mammals (birds do not hibernate). It involves much more than just going to sleep. Just going to sleep for months in bitter weather would merely be suicide for a warm-blooded animal. It involves, in fact, radical changes. The whole thermostatic heating system must be dismantled, and the stove put out.

On getting up in cold weather I have heard people complain and ask why they cannot hibernate like the animals and pass the cold of winter in a warm, snug bed. Actually, the hibernators are about as snug as a corpse and neither their nests nor bodies possess any warmth. Indeed, when they settle down to this winter sleep they go as near to death as it is possible to go and yet survive. They cease even to breathe and their internal temperature is practically the same as that of the outside air.

What prompts animals to hibernate? Why do they hibernate at all? It is generally thought that they do so to escape the cold and that the urge is put in motion by the first chill of winter. This is not so; hibernators often retire to their winter quarters during an autumn heat wave and emerge during one of those periods in early spring that we know only two well, when the cold seems worse than at any time before and snow is on the ground.

Their object is to escape starvation. We ourselves store grain and fodder to tide us over the dearth of winter, but, in the colder climes, when winter sets in most wild animals face a dreadful prospect—a barren, frozen waste without, it

Cold Operations

would seem, one particle of food anywhere, and in conditions when their systems require more food, not less. That the birds and four-legged animals (except rats and mice, who are sheltered and subsidized by man) manage to survive is always a mystery to me. Although there seems to be none there must be some food somewhere, but the competition for it must be intense. The death rate, of course, is high but the survivors start the ball rolling again.

The hibernating animals dodge these harsh and dangerous conditions by enabling themselves to live without eating anything during the whole winter. But to do this they have to become cold-blooded. The dormouse, the hedgehog, the bat and the rest lose their heat and when tested with a thermometer their body temperature is practically the same as that outside.

Even so, hibernating animals must have *some* food, otherwise their tissues would shrivel up and they would die. This food is supplied by fat accumulated in summer. Bears and dormice, for instance, lay on enormous rolls of fat before they retire, and those that have been unable to do so do not attempt to hibernate at all.

Even some human beings hibernate—after a fashion. In Siberia from time immemorial it was the custom for the inhabitants of certain villages to retire to a central building when winter came, taking with them wood and what bread they had specially saved. All went to sleep except one man, who kept a stove going and, after about twenty-four hours, wakened the others who then ate a small portion of the precious bread. After this all went to sleep again for another twenty-four hours, and another man took over. This continued for the whole winter, which in those latitudes was bitter in the extreme. Whether the custom prevails now I could not say.

It was not true hibernation, of course. The body temperature of the sleepers remained more or less normal, and they continued to breathe. When the cold is severe a truly hiber-

Cold Operations

nating animal stops breathing altogether. Tests have been made, though these are difficult, for interference is apt to disturb the rhythm of hibernation. It has been found that hibernating bats and marmots can live at least four hours in an atmosphere of pure carbon dioxide, though normally they, like other mammals, are soon killed by it. A hedgehog drowns as quickly as a human being, but a hibernating hedgehog suffers no harm after half an hour's immersion in water. Hibernating bats, too, can be kept under water for long periods. One of these bats when placed for ten hours in a scientific apparatus used for measuring the amount of oxygen taken from the air in breathing was found to have taken no oxygen, yet an active one used up five cubic inches in one hour.

Although breathing may stop, the heart continues to beat, but very slowly. For instance, the pulse of a marmot is normally 75 beats per minute, during hibernation it is about 5.

Digestion also ceases. The intestines no longer function; they neither digest food nor pass faeces. Indeed, a hibernating bear has its rectum completely blocked with a plug composed of pine needles. Since sustenance comes from the stored fat there is, of course, nothing to digest. It is true that dormice and their kind store some seeds or nuts in their winter nest and are supposed to wake and nibble at them during very mild periods, but it is probable that, in nature, these are consumed only after the animal has awakened in spring. Actually it is very difficult to rouse a hibernating dormouse. It prepares itself for sleep with its head between its paws and its tail curled round its body, and it can be rolled about on a board like a hoop without disturbing it. If woken too suddenly it dies. A boy I knew in my youth had a pet dormouse which escaped and could not be found. One day in winter when the governess was having a bath, loud screams came from the bathroom. The mouse had hibernated in a sponge and the governess suddenly found it swimming round her in the warm water. The governess said afterwards that she 'nearly died'. The boy did not mind about that but grieved about his mouse which *had* died, and he bitterly reproached her.

When awakening in the spring a hibernating animal begins to move its forelimbs, very slowly. Then its forequarters shiver for a long period. Shivering is a means of inducing warmth. It is the front part that warms first and this is in order that the heart may send oxygenated blood to the brain and central nervous system before demands are put in by the rest of the body.

Probably the best-known hibernators are bears, dormice, hedgehogs, bats and those popular pets, hamsters. Badgers lie up during cold periods but become active whenever the weather is milder. In colder countries they hibernate completely.

Grizzly bears hibernate only in their more northerly regions, as do the brown and black bear. They lie up in caves, holes, the roots of large trees and similar places, and have sometimes caused an unpleasant surprise to those who have come upon them unawares. If there is any food around, the males do not hibernate. The females usually have their young during their winter sleep. The female polar bear buries herself in the snow in autumn and has her baby in January whilst still buried. She emerges in the spring after more than six months' burial. Brumas, the baby polar bear that once drew such crowds of admirers to the London Zoo, was not, of course, born under such conditions, but Brumas, and others since, are exceptional; it is very rare for polar bears to have young in captivity.

It used to be thought that male polar bears also hibernated, since they disappeared at the same time as the females, but undoubtedly the bulk of them migrate south to the edges of open water.

Reptiles and amphibians hibernate automatically in

Cold Operations

winter in temperate climates. Unlike warm-blooded animals their systems have no heat regulators to be turned off. Frogs pass the winter in mud in ponds. Toads get into holes in the ground, as do snakes and lizards. Often in England in one hole or crevice there have been found several dozens each of slow-worms, adders, lizards and toads snuggling together. This defeats explanation, for lizards and toads are the favourite food of adders. Presumably the impulses of eating and avoiding being eaten no longer function in animals about to hibernate, but when spring comes and the hibernators have to leave their retreats, the toads and lizards must be shocked when they see the company they have been keeping.

Although cold slows down the body functions of reptiles and amphibians, this is not so in the case of all cold-blooded vertebrates. Salmon and trout, for instance, remain active even when the water is only a degree or so above freezing point.

Snails are peculiar in that they make a covering of lime over the opening of their shells and cement themselves in for the winter. Nothing will make them do this except at what they consider the fit and proper time. Subjected to artificial cold in summer they refuse to enclose themselves; subjected to heat at the beginning of winter they are not deceived, and cement themselves in as usual. Slugs, those pests of gardeners, get as far into the soil as they can and winter in a covering of slimy mucus.

'Hibernation' occurs in summer as well as winter. Summer sleep is called aestivation and it enables animals to tide over periods of shortage of food and water caused by heat and drought. As with hibernation the body functions of the sleepers almost cease. Aestivating frogs are often encountered in the tropics. When a pool begins to dry up the frog fills its bladder with water and swells up like a small balloon. Then it buries itself in mud and aestivates. The pond dries out and

64

7. The Common Cobra. On the alert. Paul Popper Ltd.

8. The King Cobra, or Hamadryad. Zoological Society of London.

9. The Black Cobra. Greatly feared in the East. Radio Times Hulton Picture Library.

Cold Operations

the mud becomes baked, so that the frog lies walled up in what, to all intents and purposes, is solid brick. There it must stay until the rains come—twelve months, eighteen, perhaps.

Aestivation is often more prolonged than hibernation. The record probably goes to the snail. An Egyptian land snail found aestivating was kept in a museum for four years before it returned to life.

Like frogs, some fishes bury themselves in mud when their pools begin to dry, and remain baked in hard clay until the water returns. The lung fish is an example. I once saw one released from a piece of what looked like rock. Placed in a basin of water the clay began to disintegrate, and soon the lung fish could be seen inside, making feeble movements. These movements increased until eventually the fish was free and swimming about, in spite of the fact that it had been entombed without water for nine months.

There are some puzzles connected with hibernation. One of them is why certain animals hibernate whilst others, closely related to them and living in similar conditions, do not. The hedgehog, for instance, hibernates, and hibernates profoundly, but moles and shrews, to which it is related, do not. Hares and rabbits do not hibernate, but some, particularly the mountain hare, pass the winter in bitterly cold regions. So do arctic foxes and other unfortunate non-hibernating animals that are trapped in winter for their pelts. Dormice and hamsters hibernate, but not ordinary rats and mice; slugs and snails, but not earthworms.

The biggest puzzle perhaps is the cause of the break-down of the heating system of warm-blooded hibernators, which alone enables them to hibernate at all. Research, however, is gradually throwing light on the subject. It has been known for some time that the very young (contrary to general assumption) can withstand cold better than their parents, though this applies more particularly to those young that are born blind and helpless—their heating system is undeveloped

Cold Operations

at the time of birth. So young rats (or cats) will recover even after their body temperature has been reduced almost to freezing-point, but their parents die when their temperature falls below 15° centigrade. Therefore it came to be taken as a rule that adult non-hibernating mammals cannot survive if their body temperatures have fallen below this point.

It has now been shown that this is not so. By taking certain precautions and working by stages adult rats can be cooled to near freezing-point and revived afterwards. In the experiments one of the chief difficulties was to prevent the body from resisting cold by increasing its heat output. But this and other difficulties were surmounted. Incidentally, it was found that at 9° C. the animal ceased to breathe, and at 6° C. its heart stopped beating. But even after further reduction to 2° C. it could still be revived.

The main difficulty in these experiments lay not so much in cooling the rat's body as in re-warming it afterwards. If general warmth was applied, however gradually, the demand of the tissues for oxygen was too great for the slowly recovering heart to supply, and this resulted in severe tissue damage. This trouble was finally overcome by first warming the heart region only (usually by a beam of light). The brain and central nervous system were thus oxygenated before the other tissues made any demand. This, of course, is what happens when hibernating animals awake, as has been shown before.

Cooling the body is now practised in surgical operations on human beings, particularly operations inside the heart and brain. When cooled, both heart and brain require less oxygen so that the blood flow is reduced and (amongst other advantages) almost bloodless operations are possible.

Animal cells and tissues, when removed, can withstand intense cold without harm. The ovaries of a rat can be kept at a temperature of –90° C. for over a year, and live when thawed and transplanted under the skin.

So far, however, it has not been possible thus to preserve

the whole animal. As long ago as 1766 the scientist and surgeon, John Hunter, stated that it should be possible to prolong a man's life in this way. If, he said, a man was prepared to give up what would normally be about the last ten years of his life he could be kept frozen for a thousand years, and awoken every century to hear the news. This far-seeing man's own experiments with animals eventually disillusioned him. Nor could it be done now. But on the other hand scientists can put forward no reasons why, with advanced knowledge, it should *not* be possible. So the stories of *Rip van Winkle*, and *The Sleeping Princess*, may not appear quite such fairy-tales to future generations as they do to us.

In tropical countries snakes neither hibernate nor aestivate. In high sub-tropical regions they hibernate. In Rhodesia the dry season brings cold nights (ice sometimes forming on buckets of water by the morning) and the days are often cold. This is sufficient to pursuade the snakes to get into holes and stay there, though why many of them make an annual re-union out of hibernation I do not know. But many do. Following each other's scent they trek to certain places and spend the cold season together.

When I was there I was told by natives and Europeans that snakes also joined together in large numbers in certain places at mating time and that any human being who went near that place was as good as done for. He was attacked on sight. I joined one such party. On a journey by mule, followed by a native constable leading a pack donkey, I camped one evening in a delightful glade, put up the tent and slept soundly. I struck camp in the morning and proceeded on my way. A mamba flashed across in front of me and then two more streaked off together. Every few yards there was a snake and I saw two couples locked together in the act of mating. I felt sorry for the native constable behind, leading the donkey, and turning round to look at him I saw that his face had gone a sort of ashen colour. Being mounted, I was in no particular

Cold Operations

danger, but I *did* serve as a sort of advance guard, clearing the snakes away from the natives behind. Molly, my mule, was in the greatest danger, but with feminine inconsistency this creature, liable at any time for any or no reason to 'create' and throw me over her head, affected a bored attitude and merely pricked her ears from time to time. This semi-nightmare did not last long. Snakes became fewer as we went along and soon we had obviously left the congregation. The only sympathy I got when I related this tale later was, 'Just like you to go and pick a spot like that to camp in!'

I think those snakes were members of a get-together hibernating party that was about to dissolve. Mating often takes place shortly after hibernation.

The snakes were by no means all mambas. I saw several cobras and other snakes as well. I did not observe them as I might have done; my thoughts were too much on Molly, wondering when she was going to throw me off and bolt.

7

A Potent Poison

H ow it came about that snakes manufactured poison
is a mystery. Over the periods their saliva, a mild
digestive juice like our own, was converted into a
poison that defies analysis even today. It was not forced upon
them by the survival competition; they could have caught
and lived on prey without using poison just as the thousands
of non-poisonous snakes still do. Poison to a snake is merely
a luxury; it enables it to get its food with very little effort, no
more effort than one bite. And why only snakes? Cats, for
instance, would be greatly helped; no running fights with
large, fierce rats or tussles with grown rabbits—just a bite and
no more effort needed. In fact, it would be an assistance to
all the carnivorae—though it would be a two-edged weapon
when they fought each other. But, of the vertebrates, unpre-
dictable Nature selected only snakes (and one lizard). One
wonders also why Nature, with some snakes, concocted
poison of such extreme potency.

In the conversion of saliva into poison one might suppose
that a fixed process took place. It did not; some snakes
manufactured a poison different in every respect from that of
the others, as different as arsenic is from strychnine, and
having different effects. One poison acts on the nerves, the
other on the blood.

The makers of the nerve poison include the mambas and

69

A Potent Poison

the cobras and their venom is called neurotoxic. Vipers (adders) and rattlesnakes manufacture the blood poison, which is known as haemolytic. Both poisons are unpleasant, but by far the more unpleasant is the blood poison. It is said that the nerve poison is the more primitive of the two, that the blood poison is, so to speak, a newer product from an improved formula. Be that as it may, the nerve poison does its business with man far more quickly than the blood poison. This, however, means nothing. Snakes did not acquire their poison for use against man but for use against prey such as rats and mice, and the effect on these of viperine poison is almost immediate.

As a slight complication it so happens that the two poisons are rarely quite pure. So the nerve poison of the cobras, etc. usually possesses a trace of the blood poison of the vipers, and vice versa. But it is legitimate, as well as convenient, to class the two poisons as two different concoctions.

I am going to give a rough idea of the effect of these poisons on a man. In Africa I was always told that if you were bitten by a mamba (neurotoxic poison) you died in twenty minutes, if by a puff adder (haemolytic or blood poison) you died in two hours. It is not so simple as that. The effect of the venom of one kind of snake on different people varies enormously. There are reasons for this, though they do not quite cover all the known facts. A snake may have bitten a victim just before it bites a man and have lost most of its poison, or most of the poison may be shed into a man's clothing before the fangs reach the skin. In these cases the man may suffer only temporary discomfort. On the other hand there are cases where men who have received only the slightest prick have died quickly. There *have* been cases when a venomous snake, for no known reason, has injected no poison at all.

When striking, a snake likes to hang on like a bulldog whilst its fangs pump the full dose of poison into the flesh. This rarely happens with a man, for he is usually able to beat

70

A Potent Poison

the reptile off. Even so, he must be quick. A cobra, for instance, can squirt out twelve drops of poison in a few seconds, and one drop can be fatal to an adult human being.

The injection of suitable antivenine (and there is not antivenine for *every* type of snake poison), if given in time, will neutralize any snake poison, but if (this is very rare) a fang should inject poison direct into a vein, death may occur in one minute. This, in fact, has happened.

On being bitten by a snake possessing neurotoxic poison, such as a cobra, the usual symptoms are a searing pain from the wound itself, then a weakness in the legs, gradually developing into incapability of making any movement at all. Saliva dribbles from the mouth owing to the paralysis of the muscles of the mouth. The tongue, too, becomes paralysed and the victim, though able to hear, is unable to speak. He begins to vomit, and has difficulty in breathing. This difficulty increases until he is suffocating, and finally breathing stops altogether. Meanwhile the heart has been racing on, and it continues to beat for a considerable time after breathing has stopped.

What happens is this: when the poison is injected it is distributed by the blood and attacks the nerve cells and nerve centres. It also attacks the central nervous system. Finally it paralyses the nerve centres that control breathing, and the lungs collapse. It has, however, a stimulating effect on the heart and only after the lungs have collapsed does the heart, owing to the accumulation of carbon dioxide, cease to operate. But if the poison is injected direct into a vein its transit is so rapid that the heart stops almost immediately. (Experimental animals, such as dogs, have died while the injection was actually being made, death thus occurring almost as quickly as if they had been shot through the brain.)

It is not easy to obtain data of the symptoms of poisoning by the deadlier snakes. Snakes can be made to bite unfortunate experimental animals, but these animals, whether they live or

71

A Potent Poison

die, cannot tell us their symptoms, and post-mortems get us little further. Not a few men have been bitten by the bad types of snakes and recovered, and here, one would think, would be an ideal source of knowledge. Not a bit; the majority remember next to nothing. Besides other sufferings, the subject is in a state of terror, and terrified men are not in a state of mind to note and memorize symptoms.

And one can hardly experiment on human beings. Volunteers for, say, mamba poisoning would be hard to come by. Nevertheless one brave soul *did* undergo such a test. Some time ago, a Dr. Eizenberger decided to experiment on himself. He did not propose, however, to kill himself, and used such a small dose that he thought the effect would be negligible—he could always use a larger dose if this one proved to have no effect. He took one drop of the venom of the green mamba of West Africa (*Dendraspis viridis*). This drop he diluted with ten times the quantity of water, and of this very weak solution he only injected 0·2 cc. into his forearm.

A burning sensation was felt immediately, and five minutes later there was a swelling over the puncture, accompanied by itching. Soon he knew that his nerves were affected. Ordinary everyday noises became deafening. His car seemed to make such a din, bumping and banging, and he thought a tyre must be punctured and got out to look. Saliva flowed copiously in his mouth and he felt as if he were intoxicated. Soon (about fifteen minutes after the injection) he was seized with nausea and weakness and decided the time had come to put an end to this experiment and do what he could to stop any further absorption of the venom. It was far too late, but he applied a tourniquet, cut open the swelling and soused the bleeding cut with a hot solution of permanganate.

His chin, lips and the tip of his tongue became numb. This numbness spread over his face and down his throat. His eyes and the base of his tongue became painful, and he lost all feeling in his fingers and toes. His ears started to drum and the pain and stiffness of his tongue travelled down his throat,

72

which became acutely sore. It became difficult to talk or swallow, and difficult and painful to breathe.

Alarmed and fearing collapse, Doctor Eizenberger gave himself an injection of strychnine, which had a good effect and improved his circulation.

Then his hand and forearm swelled up and the parts that had been numb became painful. After five hours a touch on any part of his body was painful, and swallowing was very difficult. But the worst was over. He went to bed and passed the night in a feverish state. In the morning his tongue and throat still pained, but these discomforts gradually passed off.

He made a complete recovery, and this is the case with all who are bitten by neurotoxic snakes and escape death. However severe the complications, if they do recover, recovery is complete—which can by no means be said of bites received from vipers.

And now to the blood or haemolytic poison, the poison of the vipers. There are many vipers, including the American rattlesnakes. All are venomous to a certain extent, but only a few are really deadly. Of these the puff adder and Russell's viper probably head the list.

Although the effects are more unpleasant, in these days of serum treatment a man has more chance with viperine poison then with neurotoxic (cobra, mamba, etc.) simply because the former takes longer to act and he has more time to get to a place where he can be given a shot of antivenine.

This haemolytic poison breaks down the blood and destroys its ability to coagulate. The blood-vessels, particularly the capillaries, are also broken down, and the changed blood oozes through the surrounding tissues, generally to a considerable extent. This occurs first at the site of puncture which becomes discoloured, swells and bleeds. As the poison spreads through the body large black or purple patches appear in various parts and blood issues from the mouth and nose. In fact, the subject appears to be the victim, not of poison but of a merciless 'beating up'. For instance, a Mr.

A Potent Poison

Wertzer in South Africa, bitten in the forearm by a haemo-lytic snake became a hideous sight with large black patches down both arms, down the thighs and over the stomach. He had a 'black eye' the size of a plate and blood streamed from mouth and nose.

Internal bleeding also occurs in the stomach, bladder and bowels; the skin becomes cold and clammy, the subject vomits continually and has no control over his bowels. Un-like the neurotoxic poison the haemolytic poison slows down the heart and death may occur in a few hours or after several days.

There is indirect danger attached to viperine poisoning; when the danger seems passed, the large blood-suffused areas of muscle may begin to mortify, causing death weeks later. And if this secondary poisoning is not fatal, pieces of flesh may slough off and come away. In Africa one occasionally meets natives with no calves, or very little, the flesh having sloughed off following the bite of an adder.

Snake venom is a clear, yellowish liquid, odourless and tasteless—and finding out that it is tasteless is not so rash as some people seem to think. In fact, anyone could drink a cupful with immunity, provided he or she did not have a sore in the mouth or a raw ulcer in the stomach. It is digested like ordinary food; only when injected is it dangerous. A certain queen was regarded as a heroine because she sucked her husband's wound when he was bitten by a snake, but there have been many more heroic actions than that. And it is not really very much use; however quickly one begins to suck, the bulk of the poison is already speeding to other parts.

Snake poison will keep for years without losing any of its poisonous properties. Dried poison kept for 32 years and then dissolved in water was found to be as lethal as the fresh product. Decomposition, however, does destroy the veno-mous properties. Venom taken from a dead snake will be as

74

A Potent Poison

potent as venom taken from a live snake, but not if the snake has begun to decompose. Fitzsimons took venom from a dead snake that had a *very* faint smell—slightly stale, one might say —and this venom injected into various animals had no effect on any of them. For this reason dried venom dissolved in ordinary water will only keep for about a month, but will keep indefinitely in glycerine.

This raises the question of decomposition in general. Tainted meat is supposed to be dangerous, yet many people eat pheasant, grouse and other game when it is practically rotten, in which state it is not only harmless but more digestible. Ordinary meat is almost uneatable when really fresh, but when well hung it becomes tender and good. And the longer it is hung the better. Most butchers nowadays do not hang their meat long enough; they like to sell it and get the money as soon as possible. I knew a butcher before the war who used to hang his meat until the carcass was black outside —and never since those days have I tasted steaks and joints so tender and delicious. In life, the muscles of all animals produce poison, which has to be continually cleared away by the blood. When we eat fresh meat we eat this poison but it may well be that the infinitesimal decomposition that goes with hanging destroys it, just as slight decomposition destroys the infinitely more potent poison of the snakes. A shark (the Greenland Shark) that lives in northern waters is used as food by Greenlanders and their dogs, but only after it has been kept until it smells. If eaten before then it is literally poisonous. I know that some people have become ill after eating tainted meat but I feel quite sure that this was not due to the meat itself but to some germ or filth introduced by flies. In any case man ought to be inured to bad meat. In his early stages the bulk of what left-over meat he was able to get must have been well-nigh rotten.

Boiling also destroys the toxic properties of snake venom; in the case haemolytic venom in a few minutes, but with neurotoxic venom only after several hours.

A Potent Poison

The formula of snake poison is not known. It has a protein base but chemical analysis does not disclose all the agents that are present. The smaller animals are more susceptible than human beings. A Dr. Fayrer took blood from a rabbit bitten by a snake and injected it into another rabbit. That animal also died, and when *its* blood was injected into still another rabbit that one died as well.

When a snake strikes, the operation of biting is not a simple one like that of the dog, but a series of co-ordinated, synchronized processes. The fangs of a viper are retractile and normally lie in two sheaths along the roof of the mouth. Only just before striking are they brought out and erected. The poison sacs are situated on each side of the head and are connected to ducts. These ducts, however, are not joined to the fang apertures. Only when the fangs are erected do they enter the upper cavities, which they plug, like a cork plugs a test-tube. This done, the powerful muscles round the sacs contract, forcing out the poison at considerable pressure, and they go on contracting until all the poison has been forced out—provided the snake is able to keep its grip that long. The whole process is very similar to one of our own pocket hypodermic syringes. This, too, has to be taken from its plush-lined case and assembled together before the needle enters the skin and pressure is applied. Both are used only for giving injections.

The fangs of snakes other than the very numerous vipers are non-retractile. The vipers' fangs are so long and sharp that, no doubt, it would be dangerous to the owner to keep them uncased. This is considered another pointer to the more advanced evolutionary status of the vipers.

So far we have studied the effect of bites from the dangerous snakes. What about the cures? As all know, the injection of antivenine is the answer. But this remarkable serum is a comparatively new thing. When I first went to Africa it was

76

A Potent Poison

unknown. What did we do then when we, or somebody else, received a bite from a snake? We did a lot of things—most of them very foolish things.

Returning from a patrol in my early days in the Rhodesian Police, I found the sergeant and a trooper walking another trooper (who was stripped to the waist) up and down the barrack-room. A bottle of whisky stood on a table and the sergeant held a glass of neat whisky in his hand, which he put to the escorted trooper's lips every now and then, trying to force him to drink the spirit. The patient (whom I will call the trooper who was being thus treated) seemed much upset and was exhausted. The sergeant and the other trooper were also exhausted and welcomed my arrival, the sergeant conscripting me to take his place while he had a breather. They told me the patient, while climbing a kopje, had been bitten in the arm by a big brown snake, which the sergeant thought must have been either a black mamba or a puff adder (though no two species are more unlike). The wound looked bad, but that was because it had been cut about with a knife and crystals of potassium permanganate rubbed in. A handkerchief had been tied round the arm above the wound. Now, said the sergeant, the only hope of saving the man's life was to keep him moving and make him swallow a bottle of whisky neat. Otherwise, once he lay down, he would go into a coma and would never wake. More than half a bottle of whisky had already gone.

I joined in this life-saving with enthusiasm. I was young and new to the country and felt I was learning something about the treatment of snake bite which might well come in useful later. So I and the other trooper dragged the unfortunate patient up and down, up and down. The weather was hot and the tin-roofed barrack-room like a furnace. We got him to swallow some more neat whisky, but he was getting more and more difficult, and his language ill became one who might, presumably, be called upon to meet his Maker at any moment.

77

A Potent Poison

In the end he refused to walk and we were dragging him along like a sack of mealies. This could not go on, so we had to put him on his bed, though the sergeant feared the worst since he had only drunk little more than half the bottle of whisky. Strangely enough, the patient was not drunk. I am sure of that. Though his language was wicked he did not slur his words. He fell asleep (fell into a coma, the sergeant said) and awoke at midnight to indulge in long bouts of vomiting. Vomiting, of course, *is* a symptom of snake-bite, but it is also a symptom of drinking more than half a bottle of whisky neat.

He was very ill in the morning, but more as if he had an outsize hangover than anything else. Apart from a bad temper and a consuming thirst he was fit enough by the afternoon. The sergeant said the walking and the whisky had saved him.

I quite believed him and, as I have said, treasured this lesson in life-saving. I know now that everything we did was a classic example of what *not* to do and that, had he been bitten by a poisonous snake, our treatment would have destroyed whatever chances of recovery he might have had. To list our crimes: (1) After snake-bite, rest is the first essential. Exercise drives the infected blood more quickly through the body to the heart and the nerve centres. (Presumably the sergeant had narcotic poisoning in mind.) (2) Alcohol does the same thing. Fortunately, with snake-bite, alcohol usually lies in the stomach and is not absorbed. The patient is in a state of fright and frightened people cannot digest or absorb food or alcohol. But the time comes when the alcohol *is* absorbed, and the result may be spectacular unless the patient has vomited it up beforehand. (3) Potassium permanganate crystals rubbed into freshly cut flesh are dangerous to the tissues. In any case they do no good, as many tests have shown. Nevertheless it is a recommended treatment even today. (4) A tourniquet tied between the wound and the heart is also a recommended treatment even today. It is difficult to imagine what good it can do. It has to be loosened every fifteen minutes or so, otherwise the whole limb below may mortify. In the case of the trooper related above I cannot remember that the handkerchief was once loosened. Luckily for him it must have been loosely tied in the first instance. A tourniquet only delays things slightly. When it is loosened, as it has to be from time to time, the venom sweeps through with the blood to other parts, even if it has not squirmed its way there already. Indeed, Fayrer has shown that even immediate amputation of a bitten limb fails to prevent the venom entering the blood-stream.

But, as I say, we thought we had done the right things, and we celebrated our patient's recovery on what remained of the bottle of whisky.

Lieutenant-Colonel Charpurey, a great Indian authority who has dealt with many cases of snake-bite, lays down that if a patient becomes violent he has received no poison, and that if he faints (generally supposed to be 'coma') it is due purely to fright and the snake that bit him may well be harmless.

A bottle of whisky and friends to walk one about were not usually available on a solitary patrol in the veld, so we were always supposed to carry a phial of potassium permanganate crystals and a sharp knife. I have commented on this treatment already. In any case, we usually forgot to carry the permanganate, for though the country was full of snakes, cases of snake-bite were very rare, owing not to the carefulness of the inhabitants but to the carefulness of the snakes.

There were other 'cures' in plenty. At almost every wayside store one might see small bottles named with such labels as *Smith's Snake-bite Specific*, *Jones's Infallible Snake-bite Cure*, *Dr. Higgin's Snake-bite Remedy*, and others. In smaller letters or in a pamphlet round the bottle would be glowing testimonials from snake-bitten people who had been saved by that particular preparation. And, make no mistake, these testimonials were, for the most part, genuine and there were people going around who invariably carried one or other of the bottles. Yet all these preparations were proved to be completely useless by F. W. Fitzsimons, director of the Port Elizabeth Museum, who experimented with them on various animals. Even when this had been made known it made no difference to the sales.

This provides a sidelight on human nature and explains why so many manufacturers of patent medicines make staggering profits. If you wish to grow rich all you have to do is to put something in a bottle (it doesn't matter what), label it as a cure for something (again, it does not matter what), advertise it everywhere and then pay your thousands in super tax.

These snake-bite specifics owed their enthusiastic recommendations not to blind faith in the statements of the manufacturers but to apparent clear proof of their efficiency. Not one man in fifty knows the different species of snakes and when a man is bitten it is immediately supposed that the snake is poisonous. *Smith's Snake-bite Cure*, or some other, is used and the patient recovers—as he would have done in any case. But henceforward, both to him and any witnesses, this specific is the one and only cure. And if the snake *was* poisonous it does not follow that the bite will be fatal. The snake may not have been one of the really deadly species, or there may have been other factors. The symptoms may be severe, but if he has taken Smith's Cure and recovers, the more severe the symptoms the more credit goes to the lucky Mr. Smith. If the patient dies, Mr. Smith need not worry, dead men tell no tales.

Ignorant white men were the chief believers in these quack cures. The ordinary kraal native would have nothing to do with them. He had his own cure, prepared by witchdoctors, and this cure was in a very different category. Far from being advertised it was kept secret and no witchdoctor ever divulged its ingredients. Nor, so far as I know, has anyone found out yet.

It acquired a great reputation. It had a number of names

10. The Phoorsa. An Indian snake. Although very small, about 20 per cent of its bites prove fatal. Zoological Society of London.

11. The Bushmaster. A large notorious snake of South America. Zoological Society of London.

12. The Texas Diamond Back Rattlesnake. The most dangerous of the North American Rattlesnakes. Zoological Society of London.

13. The Copperhead. A North American snake with an evil reputation which is not justified. Zoological Society of London.

A Potent Poison

according to the locality but it is more generally known as zibiba. In the main it is *supposed* to be prepared from the roots of a scrubby bush called inkwakivamuti. The roots were dried, ground into powder and mixed with the dried powdered spleen of a mamba. That may have been the recipe, or it may not.

This was the *modus operandi*: on being bitten by a poisonous neurotoxic snake, the wound must be scarified and the powder rubbed in. At the same time the patient must drink some of the powder mixed in warm water. The patient then vomits, and eventually goes to sleep. He sleeps for about ten hours and awakes perfectly fit.

Is it really any good? The natives, of course, say it is and give many tales. So do many Europeans, among them the late Lieutenant-Colonel Stevenson-Hamilton. He is responsible for what is now known as the Kruger National Park and has written important works on the fauna of South Africa. In fact, he is one of the greatest authorities on wild life in Africa. Here is an account he gave of a native police sergeant.

This sergeant one day walked into his office carrying the limp body of a dead mamba. Stevenson-Hamilton measured it—quite why, I do not know, to show interest, I suppose. It was seven feet long, a smallish specimen. Whilst he was measuring it, the sergeant remarked casually that it had just bitten his son, aged eight. His reaction to Stevenson-Hamilton's horror was to remark, 'It's quite all right. We had the medicine and gave it him straight away. He'll come to no harm.'

It had happened while the cattle were being dipped. A mamba, with the speed and unexpectedness that only mambas can display, shot from the grass roof of the bank shed and, seeking safety, charged through a crowd of natives, who panicked off in all directions. The only one who did not get out of the way in time was the sergeant's son, and he got bitten on the outside of his naked thigh—two deep fang

81

A Potent Poison

marks showed the place. Another native behind did not get away in time but with a lucky blow of his stick disabled the mamba before it passed him. It was then killed.

Stevenson-Hamilton inspected the child and the time, he says, was eleven a.m. The child had been sick but was now asleep. At 6.30 his eyes opened, but only the whites were showing and he was in a comotose condition. The thigh was much swollen. This condition would have been alarming to most observers, but those present were paying no attention to the child and evidently had no anxiety about him. The next day he was fit and walked back to his village some five miles away.

There are many other accounts of the efficiency of zibiba given by Europeans, but it would be wearisome to go through them.

Stevenson-Hamilton states that the natives recognize the difference between neurotoxic (mamba, cobra, etc.) and viperine poison and only use zibiba for the former. A viper bite is treated with hot poultices made of mealie meal. (Such poultices would certainly be quite useless for a puff adder bite but would suffice for the bites of many other adders that, in any case, do not cause death.)

Fitzsimons tested this famous native cure. He tested it on various animals and found it to be useless. That seems to be the end of the matter, but I am not so sure that it is. There are a few questions to be asked first and a few details to go into.

Firstly, did he use the genuine zibiba, the ingredients of which are secret? He himself states: 'From what plant or substance zibiba is prepared by the native doctors is as yet a secret which they have managed strictly to preserve.' Yet shortly afterwards he is saying of a sample he received for use, 'It turned out to be zibiba.'

For his first experiments he obtained a supply from the Hon. F. W. Reitz, 'a member of the government' who sent him a phial of 'genuine fresh' zibiba. The question is how did

A Potent Poison

he, or the Hon. F. W. Reitz, know that it was genuine. Fitzsimons examined this sample and all we learn from his examination is that 'it appears to be the root of a plant, finely pulverized'. Not a very satisfying analysis.

Tests on animals brought negative results.

His next supply of zibiba came from a 'well-known gentleman in Natal' who stated that he had witnessed cures on both men and animals and that he 'knew' his supply to be zibiba, though he did not mention its source. The result of Fitzsimons's tests of this were also negative.

The next donor was a 'prominent farmer in the Transvaal'. All the farmers, said he, carried this powder and believed the substance to be a certain cure for snake-bite. Fitzsimons received the powder which, he said (as mentioned before), 'turned out to be zibiba'. How it turned out to be an unknown substance we do not know. This powder also proved valueless.

Another Transvaal gentleman then wrote to Fitzsimons suggesting (and not without reason) that the supplies he had used might not have been genuine. So he sent him some powder which he 'believed' to be the right stuff. He knew of two bites cured by it. He had just enough left for *one* cure, so he sent it to Fitzsimons for an experiment to be made.

Now although this gentleman had sent what he stated to be only enough for one treatment, the following are the experiments Fitzsimons made with it.

A tom-cat was given a *large* dose. A puff adder was then made to bite it in the leg. The wound was scarified and then rubbed *thoroughly* with zibiba. After an interval more was applied. Later, the wound was rubbed with a *third* lot. The cat died in one hour, twenty-seven minutes.

A fowl was treated next. Its leg was cut and the venom of a puff adder mixed with the powder rubbed into it. The fowl died in half an hour.

One would have thought the single dose would have been exhausted by now. Not a bit. More powder was mixed with

A Potent Poison

puff adder venom, left to stand a day, and rubbed into the cut of another animal patient. The patient died.

Nor was the powder finished yet, for, says Fitzsimons, 'Other experiments followed with similar results.'

Even now this magic cruse of powder was not at an end. Some was still left and this was mixed with the powder sent by the Hon. F. W. Reitz and a monkey made to eat some. After this it was bitten by a puff adder and the punctures 'smothered' with the mixed powders. It died in due course.

Two things stand out about these experiments which seem to nullify the conclusions made. Firstly, Fitzsimons had no proof that the powders sent to him *were* zibiba. (Native doctors do not give their cures away to all and sundry.) Secondly, for some quite unknown reason, he used only puff adder poison. Yet, according to Stevenson-Hamilton, the natives themselves do not use zibiba for viperine poisoning, realizing its inadequacy.

What is the truth? No one knows, but underlying the witchdoctors' mumbo jumbo lies a deep knowledge of herbs and other cures. I once employed a Basuto native who was an expert brickmaker. He had syphilis in an advanced stage. He went to a witchdoctor and came back in three months completely cured. Pneumonia and other pulmonary complaints are often cured very quickly. When I was in the country quite horrible wounds (one, I remember, was a man half-scalped by a leopard) were treated by plastering them with a filthy mixture of ingredients including old, mouldy cow-dung. Instead of the blood poisoning I confidently expected, most of these wounds healed in an incredibly short time. Possibly, of course, the mould contained some principle similar to penicillin, which was then unknown. We shall never know the nature of the herbal remedies of the witchdoctors. They will never divulge them. By and by, as the country is opened up, witchdoctors will disappear, and their herbal knowledge will go with them. My own belief is that

A Potent Poison

natives in the interior of Africa *did* have a cure for neuro-toxic poisoning.

Now that antivenine is recognized as the only scientific cure it may seem unnecessary to hark back to the days when it was unknown. But it is a mistake to have all one's eggs in one basket. Antivenine is not available everywhere and it can only be used within a certain time limit, so let us keep an open mind for any treatment, primitive or not, which *may* give help. Because orthodox science despises a treatment it does not follow that the treatment is useless. Harley Street is not *always* in advance of the jungle.

In South America, in the old callous days, an experiment was made by students on a condemned criminal. He was told that he was to be executed by bleeding. He was blindfolded and strapped down and scratched by a needle along one side of his neck. Then warm water was made to flow along his neck into a receptacle below. Believing it to be his blood that was flowing, the criminal got slowly weaker and died in just about the same time he would have died had the bleeding been genuine. He died of fright and auto-suggestion.

In the same way hundreds of people have died from the bites of quite harmless snakes.

Should you ever have occasion to deal with anybody who has been bitten by a snake and is in a distressed condition, and if no doctor or antivenine is available, tell him that luckily, you have a certain cure you always keep handy that has never been known to fail. (It is waste of time to tell him the snake was not poisonous—he won't believe it.) Then get some salt (or anything else), scarify the wound and rub it in. The more it smarts the better. Now make him swallow some strong Epsom salts or quinine in solution (anything very bitter). None of these substances are the slightest use medically, but if the snake was non-poisonous (as is probable) he will recover quickly without the complications induced by fear and auto-suggestion. If the snake was poisonous a sense

85

A Potent Poison

of security will enable his system to cope with a condition that would have handicapped it had fear paralysed its functions. Should the snake have been one of the few really deadly ones he will have no hope, but at any rate you will have done him no harm.

This sort of thing is duplicity, of course, but duplicity is often a virtue. No doctor worth his salt does not practise duplicity at times. When travelling in the interior of China I once had to go to a mission hospital for an operation following a gun wound. I knew the doctor well and had stayed at the mission before. It was a small affair and I was soon walking about with a bandage. Then, one afternoon, a Chinese shopkeeper arrived escorted by wife and two or three others. He was moaning and hardly able to walk. His wife was moaning too. Eastern fatalism was entirely lacking in this case. He had been bitten by a snake and his friends wanted the doctor to give him the 'new' treatment (antivenine). The doctor said he would do so straight away and the patient was put to bed and an injection given. After that the patient went to sleep and everybody was happy. I was sitting in the doctor's living-room when he came in and rang up the hospital of a large Chinese town asking them to send some antivenine as soon as possible, since he had none. He added further instructions. As he put the receiver down I said, 'But I thought you'd just given him some?' The doctor smiled and shook his head. 'What he got was an injection of distilled water. He's quite all right now and fast asleep. I'll give the antivenine when it comes—if he needs it.'

I said I supposed it was a harmless snake. He said he doubted it, for there were fang marks and a large swelling. It was probably, he said, some species of viper, but so long as the patient did not worry he would come to no harm. Nor did he. He left the next day, and without his injection of antivenine, which arrived after he had gone.

What *is* this antivenine?

86

A Potent Poison

When some harmful agent, such as poison or bacteria, is taken in, a man's system immediately manufactures a substance to resist or destroy it. This is called an antibody. Unfortunately, the system cannot manufacture sufficient antibody and cannot manufacture it quickly enough to cope with the poison of a virulent snake. But when all is over, and assuming that the man has recovered, his system is fortified by the antibody created and if another snake of the same type bites him his resistance will have been increased. Therefore if a man is given, at intervals, increasing doses of the poison he will end up by being unaffected by the bite of a snake that would have killed anyone else. There are undoubtedly Indian snake charmers that have become thus immunized—though not many. But all this would be a cumbersome and painful way of immunizing a human being. Moreover, having gone through all this with, say, cobra poison the irony of fate would probably ordain that the human being would be bitten by a viper and get no assistance from his hard-won immunity to neurotoxic poison.

Similarly, any animal can be injected with increasing doses of venom and acquire increased resistance. So it occurred to two doctors that the blood of an animal made resistant to the venom of a snake might confer resistance to human beings who were bitten.

It was, of course, extremely doubtful. The animal would have acquired its resistance the hard way and over a long period. Would a small dose of its blood have any effect on the system of a completely non-resistant man after he had been bitten by a snake and the poison was already coursing through his veins? It was expecting a lot. An opium addict, for instance, can swallow enough opium to kill ten ordinary men, but a few cc. of his blood injected into a man who had taken an overdose of opium would not save him.

Undaunted, however, Doctors Fayrer and Calmette (quite independently) began experiments on these Pasteur-like lines. It was a tedious business. A small dose into some animal, then a long wait, then another *slightly* larger dose. Boring, but rather interesting, for as time went on they found they were able to inject into their subject an amount of snake venom a hundred times greater than the normal lethal dose.

But that had been more or less known already. The crucial stage had now arrived.

First (it is Dr. Fayrer's experiments of which we have knowledge), equal quantities of snake venom and the blood-serum of an immunized animal were mixed together and injected into an animal. No ill effects followed. Clearly therefore in a test-tube the serum destroyed the poisonous qualities of the venom. How about when the two met inside a body? The doctor injected the serum into an animal and, later, injected snake venom. The snake venom had little effect. The all important question now was, would the serum have effect *after* an animal had been bitten by a snake?

Contrary to the opinion of most, scientific research is, on the whole, a dull, routine job. It is rather like that of an old-time gold prospector who might wash samples for years without ever coming across a trace of 'colour'. About the beginning of this century an apparent cure for syphilis was discovered and great was the rejoicing. Some people in Paris made a gala night of it. But its name tells a story. It was called 606, which means that 605 preparations had been carefully thought out and painstakingly tested before they were found to be useless. But the thrill when 'ore' is struck (if it ever is) compensates for all that has gone before. Without scientific frustrations we would hardly have a cure for any illness nor any useful chemical process. No penicillin, no washing soda.

Antivenine, however, did not have to have a number. When the final test came and a few cc's of the serum were injected into a subject that had previously been injected with snake venom, the serum was found to arrest further development of the poison. Antivenine, the perfect cure for snake-bite had arrived.

A Potent Poison

There were snags, however. Snake poison is quick-acting. A subject bitten by a dog infected with rabies has time to go to some centre far away where the appropriate serum is kept. A snake-bitten subject has no time to make long journeys. If he does not himself carry about a supply of antivenine together with a hypodermic syringe (which few people do) he has to find a doctor quickly and although all doctors ought to possess the serum, not all of them do. For antivenine only checks *further* damage by snake poison; it does not cure damage already done. In fact, it does not destroy all the venom, but it destroys enough, if given in time, and also enables the body to develop its own antibodies capable of dealing with the remainder. It is not always infallible. There have been instances of antivenine administered an hour or so after a cobra bite failing to stop death.

Another snag is that antivenine has to be prepared from one type of snake poison only and administered only to people bitten by that particular kind of snake. Viper antivenine, for instance, is quite useless in the case of neurotoxic poisoning. There are antivenines that are, so to speak, mixed, but larger amounts must be given and too large an injection of antivenine may result in protein poisoning.

The usual dosage is 100 to 300 cc. Equally large amounts would have to be added to be sure of coping with other possible venoms. The Institute of Sero-therapico at Sao Paulo in Brazil produces five types of antivenine; for Bothrops, for South American rattlesnakes, for Bushmasters and for Coral snakes, while the fifth is a combination of these in case the identity of the snake is unknown. In North America only one serum is usually on tap, for use with rattlesnake, copperhead, and moccasin poisoning. Coral snakes, with their neurotoxic venom, are so rare that their poison is not specially catered for.

Unfortunately, antivenine, unlike anti-tetanus or antidiphtheria inoculations, or ordinary vaccination, does not confer immunity for long. Every day its effect grows weaker and in two or three weeks is almost gone. It is, in fact, a cure and not an immunizing agent.

Although it is probably not going to be used, antivenine is a serum that has to be available at many places. Therefore large amounts have to be made which means that a large animal must be selected to manufacture it; one from which good supplies of blood can be drawn. The animal chosen was the horse. This long-suffering creature, who throughout the ages has had every occasion to regret his association with man, has now to play the part of a living laboratory and in doing this has saved many human lives. He is injected with increasing doses of snake venom, each causing much discomfort, until saturation-point has been reached and he is in a position to ignore any number of bites from the most virulent of snakes. He is then bled. The blood runs into sterile containers and is allowed to clot. A clear liquid rises to the surface. This is the serum, the antivenine, and it is carefully decanted. Suitably contained, it keeps from two to three years, but loses some of its efficiency if kept in a warm place.

The equine production of antivenine is now running smoothly. It is not, however, always quite so smooth for the horse. Apart from the reactions he suffers after each dose (and several horses die, however carefully the doses are measured) horrible ulcers sometimes form at the seat of the injection. And occasionally a peculiar thing happens. A physiological change may come upon a horse that has been immunized to withstand the poison of twenty cobras or more at a time. It suddenly becomes susceptible and will succumb to a dose of poison that would hardly kill a rabbit. The reason for this change is unknown, though similar sudden allergies are well known to doctors.

8

The Constrictors

——◆~∿∪∿∪∿◖◍◗∿∪∿∿◆——

So much for the general characteristics of snakes, we might now have a look at a few individuals. It is said that the pythons are the original ancestors of all snakes, so we will begin with them and their kind. Also, being the heavyweights of the snake world they deserve first place.

As everyone knows, they are non-poisonous and kill their prey by constriction. There are two claimants for the Heavyweight World title, America with the Anaconda and India with the Reticulated Python. Both are massive (weight about 18 stone) and both *may* occasionally reach a length of 30 feet, but since there is a reported record of an anaconda of 33 feet (and a very doubtful one of 40 feet from Brazil) I think we must give the verdict to America. In general, it is very rare for either of these snakes to exceed 25 feet.

The anaconda is a boa and its other name is the Water Boa. The famous Boa Constrictor, that star turn in boys' adventure stories where it is depicted squeezing men and horses to death, is about ten to twelve feet long and lives chiefly on rabbits, birds, mice and rats. It is timid and invariably tries to escape when a man gets anyway near, but, strangely enough, the natives regard it with the utmost horror. Natives usually are great naturalists and observers and valuable sources of information about wild life generally, but when it comes to snakes they go all to pieces. They re-

91

gard the boa constrictor as poisonous and deadly and if one is detected coming towards a village the inhabitants decamp and go and live in the woods. Curran relates how a boa constrictor entered a village in Colombia at dusk (probably in search of chickens) and how all the villagers fled. This quite suited the boa, who made itself at home and even used the bed of a villager to sleep on. A white man was approached and asked to shoot it. He did, but even then for some time the villagers would not return. They said the boa's mate would come in search of it (natives seem to regard the fidelity of snakes as much higher than their own).

This is paralleled by the behaviour of the inmates of a school in India. A cobra was seen on the premises and the school closed itself down. The cobra was found and shot but the scholars and teachers would not return. They said it must have a mate. The solution in this case was easy. The shooter possessed the dead body of the cobra he had shot, so he said he would go in search of the mate. A shot rang out and the shooter produced the 'mate', which, of course, was the original cobra. Everyone was pleased and the school resumed its normal functions.

However small it may be, however harmless and however virtuous, no snake would appear to be exempt from human detestation. There is an earth snake in India a few inches long that burrows in the ground, is blind and lives on worms. A naturalist was studying these earth snakes and one day a native woman saw him with a specimen in his hand. She backed and screamed and when she had recovered sufficiently told him that everyone knew that that particular snake, if given a chance, made itself into a knot round a man's wrist so tight that the hand had to be amputated. The naturalist, by the way, had been handling these snakes for months.

This little snake, however, *is* a bit of a twister. On one occasion a chicken was found lying helpless on the road. The cause was found to be an earth snake coiled round its feet. How this came about is not known. Worms are its largest

The Constrictors

prey and it swallows them whole, squeezing and spitting out the mud. Perhaps the chicken had tried to take its worm—or even mistaken it for a worm itself.

The boa constrictor and the cobra instanced above are only two examples of the hysteria induced in human beings by snakes. Someone, I forget who, once suggested a reason. Man attributes to snakes the power of creating dread amongst other animals. This is because he feels dread himself. Most other animals have no dread of snakes. Various animals were once introduced to a python in a cage. Rats scampered over the reptile and then sat down and cleaned their faces, chickens hopped about and took grain from between its coils. Other birds did the same, except a crow who seemed for some time a bit apprehensive. In fact, the only animals who *are* terrified at the mere presence of snakes are monkeys. They scream and shriek and dash about and hurl themselves from great heights. The reason suggested why man so often behaves with somewhat similar hysteria is that he is descended from monkeys and inherits their traits.

Although the unblinking stare of a snake has no hypnotic power over the bulk of animals, it seems that on occasions it has such a power in the case of man. At any rate Fitzsimons tells of a walk he took with a friend. The friend walked ahead, and later Fitzsimons came upon him standing rigid, his protruding eyes on those of a cobra that was reared up in front of him. Fitzsimons shot the cobra and then took his still rigid friend by the arm. The man shuddered and fell down in a heap. He explained afterwards that he suddenly came upon the cobra, semi-erect and staring at him, and remembers nothing else. The cause, of course, might not have been the hypnotic power of the snake's eyes but just plain fright, the man being a newcomer to the country.

The boas belong to South America, though there are two small species, the Red Earth Boa and the Black Earth Boa, that live in India. The python inhabits Africa, India and Asia. The anaconda and the pythons are very fond of water

The Constrictors

and nearly always live near pools or streams, and may spend the day practically submerged. The larger animals, which they prefer as food, are usually taken at water holes when they go down to drink.

A man nearly lost his life through the python's love of water. In India, natives often go fishing in plantation dykes and streams. The fish here get into submerged holes along the bank, where they lie up. The fisher puts a net over the hole and twists a stick about inside. Out comes the fish and is captured. On one occasion a fisher thus employed saw what he took to be a large fish moving along the bed of the stream. He immediately put his foot on it to try and bag it, and the next instant a python had shot its coils round him up to his waist. The man held the head away and screamed for help. Though it was only a small python he could do nothing to free himself. Luckily, a plantation worker heard him and came running up. Luckier still, he carried a sickle. With this he cut the snake in half, though by the time he had done so the fisher was unconscious. He was taken home and lay in bed for three months completely paralysed. Then, strangely, he recovered and became quite fit, though not so keen on fishing as he had been.

This incident is a good illustration of the terrific muscle power of snakes. The python was only nine feet long, yet in a short time, by mere pressure, it paralysed a man for three months.

Pythons visit the plantations in numbers in the wet season and are welcomed by the managers, if not the workers, because they keep down the rats, which do enormous damage.

Normally a python never attacks a man, but if held down (as in the case above) the throwing of its coils is automatic, and once it has coiled itself hardly anything will persuade it to loosen its grip. If the python is small a man *can* be freed by a friend if the friend seizes the python's tail and uncoils it, like uncoiling a piece of string wound round a stick, but

The Constrictors

no man would have the strength to do this in the case of a large python.

Snake charmers (though not those of the *élite*) often use small pythons for their acts. These have the advantage of being non-poisonous, but all the same the charmers run a considerable risk. That is why their hands are always on the move, apparently charming by gestures but really on the alert to forestall the first sign of coil throwing. If the snake *did* succeed in this the charmer would probably be done for. His audience would never realize that this was not a part, and a good part, of his act, and in any case he has probably informed them that the snake is deadly poisonous, so there would be no rush to give him assistance.

The small pythons used by snake charmers are usually very docile and their occasional effort at constriction merely reflex actions. But one never knows. A charmer in India was putting his pet back in its cage when suddenly he found himself encoiled, while the next second the snake buried its teeth in his face. His cries brought assistance and the reptile was uncoiled, but part of its jaw had to be broken to get its body away, and after that the jaw had to be extracted by a surgeon. Possibly the man had knocked the snake's head when putting it back.

I have mentioned before the alleged breaking of bones by the constriction of a python. If a python could secure some purchase, such as a tree, against which to crush its victim then, undoubtedly, bones might be broken. But it never does. The constriction of a python is evenly distributed and death comes quickly from heart failure. In certain cases further constriction may be employed to make a sort of sausage shape of the animal for convenience in swallowing, and then bones are often folded into unusual position, but so far as I am aware there are no authentic records of broken bones. Yet even experts seem to take it for granted that bones *are* broken.

A 15-foot python was once discovered with its middle

The Constrictors

distended to an amazing degree. It was shot, and inside was found the body of a monitor 6 feet long. The monitor is a land lizard nearly as big as a crocodile. It has large teeth and claws and a row of horns along its back. It is a formidable beast and the python must have had to exert all its strength to constrict it. The gastric acids of the python had hardly begun to act on the horny hide of the monitor, but its body had begun to decompose in the stomach and was swollen out like a balloon. After the gas had been let out its girth was found to be 25 inches. In spite of the great pressure to which it must have been subjected no bones were broken.

Another python was found to have swallowed a full-grown Barking Deer. This animal is about the size of a roe buck with rather delicate limbs, but here again a thorough examination was made, and no bones had been broken.

Once, in India, a Captain Smith of the forest service left his tent to go for a walk with his spaniel. The dog ran on ahead and suddenly loud yells were heard. Captain Smith rushed up and found his dog behind a bush in the coils of a python. The dog was completely enveloped in coils and only a small portion of its hindquarters was visible. By beating savagely with a heavy stick the python was made to uncoil itself (a thing it rarely does). The dog was streaming with blood from its mouth, but nevertheless wished to return and fight the python. A few more blows killed the python (or seemed to) and it was found to measure 11 feet. The dog was comparatively unhurt and, of course, no bones broken. As a postscript, the dead snake was dragged to the Captain's tent, who then decided to go in and make a cup of tea before skinning it. In the middle of drinking the tea his boy came in and told him that the snake had gone. After a search it was found in the act of taking a chicken! That snake must certainly have been both tough and hungry.

On the other hand a big-game hunter, who wrote a few books some time ago describes how he heard the yelling of a native dog and went to the rescue. He found it in the coils of

14. The Fer de Lance. A dangerous inhabitant of tropical America.
Paul Popper Ltd.

15. Russell's Viper with three-day-old young. Notorious as a death dealer in India. Paul Popper Ltd.

16. The Puff Adder. Lethargic but deadly. Common in South Africa. Paul Popper Ltd.

17. The Night Adder. A common South African snake. This is another of the many snakes that have unjustly acquired evil reputations. Zoological Society of London.

The Constrictors

a python, which he killed. The dog was *in extremis* and, went on the author, 'every bone in its body was broken', a statement so obviously untrue that one wonders if any were broken at all.

In short, the python's aim is not to inflict savage internal breakages but to stop the heart by pressure.

I know of no case of a man having been killed by a python, though if man were in the habit of drinking at water-holes at night it might be a different matter. Children, however, are in a different category, and many native children have undoubtedly been taken from time to time. If swallowed by a python there would be no clue to their disappearance. Fitzsimons gives an account of a native boy in Africa who used to spend a lot of time playing in the reeds near his kraal. One day he was missing. The next day a python was found lying up, and despatched with knobkerries. It was cut open and the body of the boy was found inside.

Although pythons are not venomous they possess formidable teeth and can inflict nasty bites. They never use their teeth unless cornered, and the reticulated python never uses them at all on man. It is timid and, like the ostrich in sand, hides its head in its coils when a man approaches. This is fortunate, for many collectors treat it almost with contempt, yet with its great size and strength any man would be powerless if it chose to be aggressive.

It is by no means so diffident with the prey it takes for food. A 6-foot panther was found inside one python. Full-grown tigers are said by the natives to be taken quite often, though I know of no authentic records of this. Of course, at a water-hole they probably throw their coils round anything that comes along, and hope for the best.

Mistakes must often be made by pythons and boas. Their eyesight is poor (and in any case they usually operate at night), their hearing confined to ground vibrations, their sense of smell small, their sense of taste almost non-existent (a python once swallowed a rug which had been used by a

97

dog for a bed). It is the tongue they rely on for almost all their information and that is why they are flicking it in and out all the time even when they are not on the trail of prey.

But the tongue is of no use to pythons if they are waiting in the water. They have to act as soon as their would-be prey begins to drink, without finding out what it is. And if it is an elephant or a rhinoceros or an eland they are in for trouble. No doubt they soon realize their mistake and uncoil themselves. We do not know; no observer is likely to be present on such occasions. There is a photograph, however, of a 'mistake' in the *Bombay Natural History Journal*. It shows a python clinging round a great dead crocodile that it had constricted without the faintest hope of ever being able to swallow it.

Though a sluggish mover on land the python can whip its coils round a victim with lightning-like rapidity. It usually waits along a path or behind a bush, and when some prey comes along seizes it with its fangs and throws its coils.

The South Africa python (length from twenty to twenty-five feet) is not so placid as the larger Reticulated python. Though never asking for trouble and retreating whenever possible, it will attack a man savagely if cornered, and its teeth can inflict nasty bites. These bites as a rule do not turn septic like those of the mammal carnivorae. This is understandable; lions, leopards, etc., often chew their prey and its offal when it is putrid. In fact, a few bites from a lion, of no significance in themselves, invariably introduce poison as dangerous as that of a venomous snake. Snakes never chew their food nor do they swallow anything decomposed.

When swallowing, the recurved teeth of a snake work independently on either side. The jaws are connected by elastic-like ligatures, so that the teeth on one side push the food down and then those on the other side come into play, pushing it down farther. A kind of relay work.

The usual belief that a python is quite helpless after

The Constrictors

swallowing a large animal is not entirely true. Even when the prey has been swallowed for a fair period the python can eject it, though it takes some time. It is this fact that has led to another erroneous belief. When the prey is thrown up it is covered with mucus from the stomach. From time to time hunters have come upon such prey ejected by a disturbed python and have come to the conclusion that the python was about to *begin* its meal when it was frightened off. Therefore they said that a python always covers an animal with mucus from its mouth before swallowing it.

As I have said, after killing a large prey a python may constrict it again in order to get it into better shape for swallowing. The position and folding of the long legs of an antelope cut out from inside the snake show that much care has been given to the arrangement of the creature's limbs.

Boas bring forth their young alive, pythons lay eggs. The female python makes, or occupies, a sort of nest, a hollow in the ground or a disused antbear hole. In this she lays forty to fifty eggs the size of goose eggs, weighing about five ounces and containing pale yellow yolks like those of deep-litter hens. The shell is not brittle but soft and leathery. The site must be moist. The mother coils herself round them so that none is visible. It takes nearly three months for them to hatch and during this time the python does not eat nor, it is said, drink. The eggs are never left except for an occasional female who goes off at night to have a bath. The python cannot be said to 'incubate' her eggs, for she has no warmth. Her sitting is probably to protect them from enemies and to prevent them from drying up in the sun.

A fast of three months, however, means nothing to a python. In a Paris reptile-house a python fasted for two and a half years and seemed none the worse for it. One wonders, therefore, whether the forced feeding so assiduously and laboriously practised in many reptile-houses and snake parks is really necessary; the time generally comes when the python decides to start eating again. In India a snake lover had a

The Constrictors

captive 8-foot python that had fasted so long that it was nothing but skin and bone. Then, at the end of November 1926, this snake (like some human slimmers) suddenly decided that fasting was not worth while, and tucked its bib in. During December it ate 16 rats, 1 cane rat (not a rat at all but a creature about the size of a beaver) and 1 guinea-pig. In the following year it ate 15 rats, 7 cane rats, 20 guinea-pigs, 3 sparrows, 1 wagtail, 3 screech owls, 8 crows, 1 sparrow hawk, 1 seven-foot rat snake, 1 koel and 1 parrot. The records only go on now until 18th March 1928. In this two and a half months it ate 5 rats, 5 crows, 3 guinea-pigs, 1 enormous bandicoot, 1 large rabbit and 2 kites. Some of these were taken alive, some dead.

This python, judging by its size, was a youngster. Even so, comparing it with a human child, its meat intake may not seem anything out of the way. But a python, unlike a child, does not have to take in food for warmth. Also everything in the animal it eats goes for nourishment. When we eat a rabbit we first throw away a considerable part of it: the skin, head, feet and guts. With a chicken or a pheasant the waste is more or less the same. And then, when it comes to table, we leave all the bones. A snake eats and digests the whole carcass and so gets 100 per cent more value from it. If we could do this, how the cost of living would go down! And it would go down still further if we could fast as long and comfortably as a snake. One begins to wonder, really, whether our interior stoves are worth their running expenses.

Among domestic animals dogs and goats are the chief victims of pythons. Cats are rarely taken, but a large reticulated python when killed and cut open was found to contain the semi-sacred body of one of the King of Siam's royal cats—together with its silver bell. Presumably the cat had been constricted, though it must have presented difficulties to a large python; perhaps, like a rat, it had been killed by the first bite. A dog, a goat and a child are the ideal size for a grown python.

The Constrictors

In the advertisements of a certain Sunday paper there is a section entitled 'For the Gourmet'. Here many unusual foods are offered; insects, including ants, grubs of various kinds, snails and frogs of course, and others, but I have never noticed python. Yet I once grilled a steak from a python of about seven feet long over the camp fire and found it delicious—like chicken. Nor, incidentally do porcupines appear in these advertisements, but when I tried the meat of a half-grown porcupine in Africa it was excellent, a kind of blend of pork and chicken. I wish porcupines *could* become a popular dish. I am all for getting rid of them. Their spines inflict lingering agony on a host of animals and they will attack dogs and other creatures without the slightest provocation. But they are nocturnal and very cunning and possess an uncanny sense of detecting traps.

I must add to this paragraph on food that I have recently been told that in America they are now canning rattlesnakes.

When the snake discarded its legs and elongated its body it did so to assist motion. By a pure fluke its new type of body gave it another advantage; it presented the snake with a new method of killing possessed by no other animal, and the snake was not slow to adopt it. Killing is an art; to the carnivorae it is an essential art, it is their means of subsistence. The lion is probably the foremost master, adroitly breaking the neck even of heavy beasts. Cheetahs, leopards, tigers are similarly talented. Those successful hunters, the wild dogs of Africa might appear to have no art at all. They take haphazard running bites at their prey. But they do have art, and this appears in the way they run down a selected prey by relays, one team taking over from another. Man is the only meat-eating animal who has no natural killing weapons. So in very early days he must have been a vegetarian, apart from scraps of rotten meat he found or small birds or rodents he managed to catch with his hands. All this changed when he invented weapons, slings, spears, etc. and traps, and he then entered the field as a killing artist.

101

The Constrictors

Art gave way to certainty when modern rifles came into use, the only artist being the gun-maker. Man now possessed the means of killing any animal that walked the earth. And he did kill most of them. The occasional fatalities that happened to big-game hunters took place because they could not use properly the invincible weapons they possessed—they did not shoot straight.

By employing constriction the snake avoided any danger of damage or death in a savage fight. (You will recall the python that swallowed a 6-foot panther without receiving a scratch or bite.) Once the coils are thrown, the prey is trussed up as if by ropes, and once the tremendous pressure comes into play unconsciousness follows quickly. An equally comfortable and safe way of killing, of course, is used by the bite of poison-injecting snakes, but theirs is not an 'invention'; other animals use it too.

9

Notorious Characters

———•⌇⌇⌇⌇⌇⊙⌇⌇⌇⌇•———

I have no intention, even if I could, of dealing with all the species of snakes. There are more than 2,000 species in the world so it is impossible even to mention quarter of them, unless one just writes out a catalogue. But one must have some sort of a plan and I propose to deal with a few of the better known snakes. And the better known snakes, of course, are the wicked ones. The good, useful, harmless snakes make no appeal to the average man, though they outnumber the others many-fold. It is the same with our own human specimens; almost everyone is interested in murderers, but few in virtuous men. Madame Tussaud can charge an additional fee for seeing the former, but bishops, missionaries and reformers can be viewed without extra charge.

I will deal first with selected members of the snakes that inject poison that affects the nervous system. Heading the list is the virulent, venomous Mamba of Africa. It was once supposed that there were two mambas, the green mamba and the black mamba, the green mamba being a tree snake, but it is now fairly certain that both (in South Africa at any rate) are varieties of the same species. When it is young, and up to about seven feet in length, the mamba is greenish. As it grows older and longer its colour changes to dark olive and sometimes black. It also becomes more terrestrial. The black mamba, of course, is the more dangerous of the two because it is larger and therefore its bite more venomous.

A mamba is very thin and long but exceedingly graceful. When it glides along, its head and part of its front slightly elevated it represents the beauty of motion. It seems to be swimming swiftly through grass.

Besides being the most venomous, it has the reputation of being the most aggressive of snakes. Curran and Kauffeld in their book on snakes state, 'The more familiar one becomes with the habits and characteristics of most poisonous snakes the less one fears them, because very few are really dangerous. This, however, is not true of the black mamba. There knowledge breeds even greater caution.'

Fitzsimons in one of his books gives hair-raising tales of reigns of terror by mambas; mambas that established themselves in certain places and attacked anyone who came within sight, so that no one dared to go within quarter of a mile of their strongholds. Tales also of unmolested mambas pursuing, overtaking and killing men, apparently from sheer love of slaughter. I feel somehow that Fitzsimons, great authority though he was, failed to take the necessary pinch of salt with these stories he was told. Very sad is his tale of a boy who went daily from a farm to school and one day took a short cut which passed the lair of a certain man-killing mamba. The mamba came flying out as soon as the boy was in sight. The boy bolted and somehow escaped the wicked ogre. The father (not unnaturally) on hearing of the escape forbade the boy ever again to go to school by that route. Months went by and then, in winter, the boy happened to start off late for school and decided to take the short cut. The mamba espied him and pursued. The boy ran for dear life but was overtaken, bitten, and died in a short time. This should be a very good moral tale for children and teach them always to obey their parents, but one cannot help wondering why the mamba, in winter, was not hibernating instead of expending useless energy chasing children it could not eat.

Notorious Characters

Another tale he records (told him by the father several years after the event) is that of a mamba on the prowl and *very hungry*. It saw a boy, chased and bit him and the boy died. Apart from the chasing it is the 'very hungry' that makes one smile.

I have met many mambas. On patrol in Rhodesia somehow it so happened that I nearly always met one or two, though the rest of my colleagues met hardly any. On several occasions I had what I suppose might be classed 'narrow escapes' when mambas I had disturbed flashed by, almost touching me, making for their retreats, but luckily I never received that sideway bite for which the creature is famous. My job also entailed visiting isolated farmers, storekeepers, missionaries and others and I never heard any first-hand tales of mambas *pursuing* people. All, however, never doubted the oft-told myth that a mamba can overtake a man on a galloping horse. But the mamba undoubtedly is the most aggressive of snakes, and by aggressive I mean the most apt to retaliate if it thinks itself in danger. All the other poisonous snakes, with the possible exception of the King Cobra, seek safety always in flight. Hurling stones at them merely hastens their retreat, but if a mamba is hit by a stone and hurt, it will turn round and come back to attack. Nearly all snakes are great artists at bluffing. The mamba never bluffs. If a mamba adopts a threatening attitude the only course is to blow its head off, or run like a stag.

Some indication of the high toxicity of the mamba's venom may be gathered from two incidents. A hunting party assembled in Southern Rhodesia to shoot buck. The party included eight dogs ranging from a Great Dane to a small fox-terrier. It was the fox-terrier (as usual) that began the trouble. In the long grass it suddenly started an excited yapping, which brought every dog running. The fox-terrier was fastened on to a mamba, and the rest of the pack charged into the fun Screams and yelps and pandemonium ensued, and soon the mamba was dead. So, shortly afterwards, were seven dogs, including the terrier and the Great Dane. The eighth, a mongrel (and mongrels were highly prized in those days if they were any good at hunting) was missing. The party dispersed. Two days later the mongrel appeared at a farm. The owner was notified and sent a native to bring it back to his place. It was a changed dog, however, and behaved so strangely on the way back that the native got scared and let it go. It was never seen again.

On another occasion a farmer ploughing with six oxen disturbed a mamba which leapt up the leg of the hindmost ox and travelled over the backs of the whole team, biting four oxen in the process. Two died quickly, the other two recovered after a long period.

All these bites given to dogs and oxen were quick ones. When a poisonous snake bites it likes to hang on, for all the time it hangs on more poison is pumped into the victim. So all those that died had received only a small portion of the mamba's poison.

Most snakes, when disabled, accept their fate and give up. Not the mamba. Another farmer was ploughing, and his plough cut a mamba clean in two. Interested, he dismounted and went to inspect the severed snake. The last thing he expected was trouble, but the fore half of the mamba attacked and bit him in the leg. He died in two hours.

A member of that famous football team, the Springboks, was another victim of the mamba. Out hunting with others one day in Rhodesia he disturbed a mamba, which flashed by and gave him a side bite. The bite only seemed to hit the top of his leather boot, but a small prick on his leg showed that he had not entirely escaped. He was given brandy frequently, and in all drank a whole bottle. For an hour he was in a very cheerful frame of mind, laughing and joking. Then he calmed down and became more normal except that the muscles of his mouth began to twitch and he had an attack of diarrhoea (which continued). Hours went by during which he and his friends chatted over the camp fire and discussed

106

future hunting plans. Then he became drowsy, and suddenly jumped to his feet clutching at his throat. He fell down, struggled, and in five minutes was dead.

He died six hours after being bitten. He was 21 years old and in perfect physical condition and had received only a small amount of poison. He would have lived longer and might have escaped altogether but for the brandy. His actions showed that he was not frightened (the prick being so minute). If he had been frightened the brandy would have been locked in his stomach. As it was, it worked in conjunction with the venom. An ordinary tot would probably have helped—but a whole bottle!

Practical jokers, unfortunately, are always with us. I must admit that in my youth I figured both as a victim and as a perpetrator, but it is a very primitive form of humour and I am no longer amused when anyone makes me an apple-pie bed. I once saw practical jokers discomfited twice in one evening. A new recruit for the B.S.A. Police had arrived in camp from England. He had that girlish complexion and look of child-like innocence that practical jokers find irresistible. He wrote a letter home the same day and found that he had missed the camp post. He badly wanted to catch the post and was told that he could do so if he went into the town and posted his letter there. The town was a mile away and time was pressing. What to do? He was told that the Regimental Sergeant-Major had a bicycle that he was always ready to lend. The raw youth went to his office and the practical jokers rocked with laughter, for the R.S.M. was as fierce and stern a martinet as ever existed and even junior officers quailed before him. So judge the amazement of the jokers when the new recruit came out from the veranda wheeling a bicycle! We gleaned afterwards that the R.S.M. subjected the youth to a long look. Doubtless the innocent-looking face told him the whole story, for all he said was, 'All right, it's on the veranda. Leave it there when you get back.'

Notorious Characters

Whilst he was away the discomfited jokers, smarting from their wound, put a dead snake in his bed. This I thought a bit above the odds and quietly tipped the victim off about it. So when he got into bed he said, 'Anyone lost a snake? There's one here,' and threw it on the floor. He was more or less left alone after that.

But practical jokes do not always end so well, especially when they deal with snakes, even dead ones. The following account appeared in a South African paper shortly after the event. A farmer and his friend went hunting, saw a mamba and shot it. They brought it home, dragging it by a cord. Then the idea of a nice little joke occurred to the farmer. They had entered the house by a window which entered into his bedroom, so he arranged the snake in a realistic attitude on the floor. In the living-room he asked his wife if she would go and get his pipe from the bedroom. She went, and the two waited, straining their ears for a feminine shriek. None came. After a period they went to the bedroom and found the door jammed. They forced it open and inside found a dead wife and a very live black mamba, as well as the original dead mamba. The husband managed to ward off the snake's attacks with a pillow while his friend rushed for his shotgun. The friend got back and shot the snake. What had happened evidently was that, this being the mating season, a male mamba had followed the scent of the dead female where her body had been dragged along the ground and had entered the open window. When the woman appeared the snake felt itself cornered and went straight for her. She flung herself back against the door, jamming it. In her fear she was probably unable to utter a sound. The quickness of her death might have been due to one of the snake's fangs piercing a vein, though death in ten minutes from a mamba bite is not unknown.

As I have said, I have had many mambas flash by me on the veld and so have been in possible danger, but I was never scared for the simple reason I had no time to be. Before I

108

realized a snake was coming, it had gone. On one occasion, however, I *was* scared. I was in temporary charge of the police station of Fort Usher in Rhodesia and the other two Europeans were out on patrol. Left in the camp were fifteen native police and about twenty convicts. I had a small kya (hut) as my living quarters. A new floor for this kya had just been laid down consisting of the usual mixture of powdered termite hill and cow-dung (which, incidentally, makes an excellent cork-like floor). It was still wet, so newspapers had been spread over it. I went to bed that night after shutting the door but leaving the window open.

In the early morning the convicts used to sweep the square outside with long switch brooms, and the sound of sweeping was always my alarm clock.

I was awoken next morning by the usual sweeping noise but decided to lie in a bit before getting up. As I lay there drowsily it suddenly occurred to me that it was still dark. Why were the convicts sweeping the square in the dark? I lifted the mosquito netting and from the bed lit the candle on the side table. What I saw made me dive back into bed and tuck in the mosquito-netting. A large black mamba was slithering along all over the floor and it was the rustling of the newspapers that had made the sweeping sound. The snake considered itself trapped and was alarmed and furious, and the flapping of the newspapers made it more furious still. It was obvious he had got in by the small open window which was about four feet from the ground, having climbed a honeysuckle which was trained round the outside of the window. Now he could not get out and was exploring every cranny to try and find a way and getting madder and madder in the process.

At times his head would come sliding along the base of the mosquito-netting and I blessed my lucky stars that I was using one. Had I got out of bed I would have been attacked immediately, so I just lay there. Another worry was the candle. The table was slight and low and if the snake had knocked it over it would have set fire to the mosquito-netting, and then the thatch and the whole place would have been in flames. From time to time I yelled and shouted like a fog-horn, but the native quarters were some distance away and there was no response. I could not see my watch but I judged later that it must have been about three a.m.

Never in my life have three hours passed so slowly but at last a faint light appeared at the window. It grew stronger, and then I heard the authentic sound of sweeping (mixed with that of the snake). My shouts were heard and the face of the native sergeant appeared at the window. I told him what was happening, and he emitted a horrified *A-Wa* when he saw the snake. His face disappeared for a time, and then returned. I told him to get all the police with knobkerries, sticks and assagais, then open the door and get behind it (the door opened outwards). In due course the door opened—slowly—and the mamba was out like a flash. He was followed by a shower of knobkerries and hit and hurt and seemed inclined to come back and attack. Then a long assagai, used with a sideways, sweeping motion, caught him in the neck and despatched him. He was then, amidst shouts of exultation, battered by knobkerries.

The native who got him with the assagai was one of the convicts. When I measured the body it was over twelve feet long and the colour was almost black. Normally, my dog, Sam, an enormous half-bred Irish Wolfhound, would have been with me in the hut but owing to the floor I had put him in the stables. He would certainly have killed the snake, but the snake would equally certainly have killed him.

It is impossible to give even an approximate census of the number of mambas in Africa, or the numbers of snakes as a whole. There are probably more snakes in Africa than in India, but in remarkable contrast to India's phenomenal death roll from snakes bites, such deaths in Africa are relatively few. A doctor who lived in the Congo for fifteen years stated that during the whole of that time he never

110

personally encountered a case of a death from snake-bite. Yet the Congo is the home of a large number of species.

Beyond doubt, the most notorious snake is the cobra. The very name chills the blood of those who have never seen a snake in their lives. As a boy I was given to understand that meeting a cobra meant certain death, and on that account greatly admired the bravery of missionaries who went out to India, and decided not to go there myself. I was also thrilled by pictures of eastern snake charmers in their flowing robes keeping a deadly cobra at bay by the notes of a flute. At least, I was until some know-all told me the fangs were always extracted.

The fangs are rarely, if ever, extracted. New ones grow quickly and to keep a snake 'safe' the fangs would have to be extracted at frequent intervals. The fangs are an important part of a poisonous snake's make-up and to extract them even two or three times would result in illness and infection and the snake would probably die.

A word about snake charmers. Indian snake charmers dressed in Indian robes operate in Africa, Europe and America. (They used to come regularly to police stations in Rhodesia.) They are nearly all humbugs. They use harmless snakes and state they are cobras, and since few people know a cobra when they see one they get away with it. In the Bulawayo police camp when I was there a snake charmer presented his act, squatting on the ground, and when it was half-way through, a frisky camp pup charged into him and his snake. The snake seized the pup by its thigh and was dragged about ten yards before the charmer rescued it—and departed. The pup, always boisterous, remained as boisterous as ever and never suffered the slightest ill effect.

Often the trouble for these fake charmers is to get their snakes to take any interest in the act, and not coil up and go to sleep. I remember an Indian snake charmer who had to be thrown out of the police camp for being a perpetual nuisance.

Notorious Characters

Among his belongings was a small prong, used no doubt surreptitiously to stir up his pet to show *some* sign of animation. He used to combine snake charming with conjuring acts. He used stones and did the 'go away Peter, come back Paul' kind of trick. Once, while so engaged his snake got out of its basket and sauntered off to have a look at the audience. When that particular act was over the charmer found that he had no audience, no snake and no coins on his sheet.

But the true snake charmers in India and Asia are in a very different category. The best of them are dedicated to their art and their knowledge is passed on from one generation to another. They are more skilled than any matador and can judge and avoid a snake's strike within a fraction of an inch. They deal with cobras which they catch in the jungle themselves and swear to the Snake God to release on a certain date —and this they always do, for to fail by one day, they think, would bring retaliation in the shape of a fatal bite.

There are two cobras in India, the Common or Indian Cobra and the King Cobra, or Hamadryad. The latter is the largest of all poisonous snakes (18 feet). After the mamba, it is also the most aggressive (using that term with my previous qualifications). The common cobra (the one with the famous 'spectacles' when its hood is expanded) is about as aggressive as a mouse. It seeks only escape. Yet its bite is deadly. The king cobra's venom is commonly supposed to be far more virulent than that of the common cobra, but what tests have been made indicate that the two are about the same.

The dedicated snake charmers who take a pride in their art generally use the king cobra and scorn those colleagues who perform with the common cobra. They are really snake worshippers and, as I have said, make a sort of rite in collecting their king cobras in the jungle. The initiation of a newly captured king cobra for show purposes is a fearsome thing. It is simply played with and invited to strike, which it does eagerly. A cobra can only get its bite in by a forward strike, so the trainers (often girls) can jerk their heads and hands

112

18. The Gaboon Viper. Brilliantly coloured. Commonly classed as the world's most beautiful snake. Paul Popper Ltd.

19. The Adder. Britain's only poisonous snake. Its venom is comparatively mild. Radio Times Hulton Picture Library.

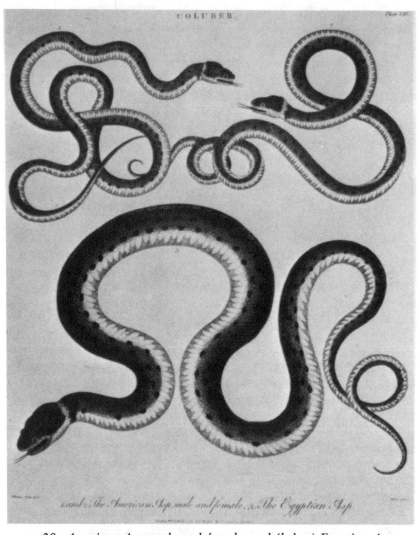

20. *American Asp, male and female, and (below) Egyptian Asp.*
Radio Times Hulton Picture Library.

away and avoid death by a hair's breadth. In time the cobra gets tired of striking at vanishing heads and hands and retires sulkily into its basket. After a course of this treatment, the dreaded king cobra, when aroused from its basket and before an audience, simply sways in front of the pipes of the charmer wondering whether to strike or not, and generally deciding it is not worth while. All the time, the charmer is taking note of every angle of the erected neck, judging precisely where a strike would land.

But onlookers sometimes see a public performance with a more or less newly captured king cobra. A colleague of mine in China saw one performed by the girl assistant of the charmer, and told me about it. She dragged a king cobra from a basket and threw it aside. It lunged at her immediately, and missed. She did not seem even to look at it, being more engaged in smiling at the audience, but a movement to one side left the snake with its fangs embedded in her white robe. Without even looking, she grasped the reptile by the neck and laid it in front of her. It was full of fight and evidently considered this girl a dangerous aggressor. It struck repeatedly. She invited it to strike (which is probably the safest thing to do if you know how to judge these things). How crude is the performance of a matador compared with this!

It has been recorded that at times some of these girl charmers creep gradually towards a king cobra and kiss it on the mouth. Well, there are many ways of earning a living but that is not one which would appeal to me.

Although, so far as I know, there are no authentic instances of a hamadryad (to ring the changes on the name) attacking a man unprovoked, there are many about hurt or wounded ones doing so. Also a hamadryad is apt to attack when disturbed 'sitting' on her eggs. At this time her mate is usually close by and if the two of them come out steps have to be taken quickly—literally, for the hamadryad is probably the fastest snake after the mamba. Those who have been chased by one have said that they had to exert all their running powers to escape. Not infrequently, in Asia, native paths have been closed because a hamadryad and her mate had eggs in the vicinity.

An instance of this snake's desire to retaliate when interfered with is provided by a Major Fraser, motoring in India with his wife. He saw a large snake crossing the road, accelerated and ran over it. But he only got the tail end. He stopped to have a look back and the next minute the snake's head appeared at the open passenger window, furiously trying to get in. The wife threw herself over on to her husband and he drove on. After a while he stopped and got out. The snake was on the road in a menacing position and as soon as he left the car it came for him. He quickly got back and into motion. They saw that the snake stayed on the road in its semi-erect position for some time, and then went off into the bush. With its sore rump it must still have been in a seething rage, and doubtless had it met any native it would have attacked at once and we would have had another story of an unprovoked attack by a hamadryad.

The king cobra must be a veritable ogre to its fellows, for it feeds chiefly on other snakes and has a hearty appetite. That it lives *entirely* on snakes, as has been said, is wrong, for lizards have been found inside the stomach. I presume if snakes were in short supply it would take anything it could get. But it certainly *prefers* snakes, for a captive specimen in Regent's Park during five months ate 82 snakes, refusing all other food including lizards, rats, guinea-pigs and pigeons.

Some coolies in Burma once had a unique chance to put on record the tale of a thrilling snake fight. They came upon two snakes in furious combat. One was an 8-foot python and the other a 10½-foot hamadryad. A deadly poisonous snake versus a heavy non-poisonous snake. The python already had the advantage; it had made a deep rent in the cobra's side and was holding on and increasing the damage without, so far as could be seen afterwards, receiving any damage itself.

Notorious Characters

And at this interesting stage the coolies stopped the fight by killing them both.

The python, so far as is known, does not ever in its native haunts feed on snakes, so the hamadryad must have been the aggressor. And hamadryads *do* eat pythons. One was killed on the Goa frontier with three feet of python already swallowed. The python was 9 feet, the hamadryad 12 feet. Whether the remaining six feet of python could have been taken in we do not know. Mr. Mervyn states he shot a hamadryad 13 feet long in the act of swallowing a python of 8 feet. A pity all these trigger-happy gentlemen could not have waited a little in the interest of knowledge.

A man once kept a black cobra as a pet. He was a Major Boyd of the R.A.M.C. stationed at Ferozepore. Not only did he give his dangerous inmate the run of the house but he treated it like a dog or cat, letting it out of the house at regular times to get exercise and fresh air. One evening, when he had let the cobra out and it was taking its exercise, he saw a small owl swoop down and give it a blow on the head with its wing. The snake adopted the usual attitude of defence, raising itself and expanding its hood. The owl hovered in front but kept out of reach. It was all part of a concerted plan, for while the snake's attention was thus engaged another owl (the mate, no doubt) flew up from behind, struck the snake on the head and knocked it to the ground. Thereafter the owls attacked in turns, knocking the snake down whenever it raised its head. Major Boyd, thinking things had gone far enough, hastened up and rescued his pet but, alas, the rescue came too late for he found that the snake's lower jaw had been fractured, and he had to destroy it. He was greatly upset, for he had had it a long time, it was very tame and he was extremely fond of it.

Like that of the mamba the venom of the king cobra acts rapidly. A man bitten by one died in a quarter of an hour and a coolie woman bitten on the thigh died in twenty minutes. So antivenine in the case of bites from these snakes is rarely

115

available. They are inflicted mostly in the jungle and it would mean a journey of several hours to get to a doctor by someone who would probably be incapable of walking in any case.

On the other hand it is on record that a Burmese snake catcher bitten by a king cobra chewed some vegetable pulp, applied it to the wound and suffered no ill effects. Possibly he had become immunized to the poison. If not, it is a pity we have no knowledge of the vegetables used.

The self-effacing Common Cobra has several redoubtable feats to its credit, or rather its discredit. One killed a tiger. It happened in a private zoo belonging to an Indian potentate, His Highness the Jam Saheb. In one of the cages was a tigress with three fine cubs. On an early morning the keeper, doing his round, found the tigress dead and a cobra peacefully asleep in a corner of the cage. It had evidently entered the cage in the night seeking rats and perhaps had been sniffed at by the tigress, who received a bite in the cheek. A gun shot settled the cobra but the cubs remained, very lively and indignant at their mother's not giving them the usual meal. The solution of the difficulty seems incredible. Goats are terrified by the smell of tiger (as are most animals) but three female goats were found that consented to act as foster mothers and took on the job conscientiously. The rough, boisterous cubs throve well on the goat milk and the mothers did not seem to resent the buffetings they got.

The enormous number of deaths from snake bites reported in India is said to be caused largely by four snakes, the Cobra, the Krait, Russell's Viper and the Phoorsa. The first two inject neurotoxic poison and the latter viperine. I am surprised at the phoorsa being included in the list for I could quote case after case of recovery from its bite both by Europeans and natives. The bite, however, is apparently very painful. The native servant of a government official was bitten by one and his master made four cuts in the skin and pulled the flaps out. Into the surface of flesh thus exposed he rubbed neat crystals of permanganate of potash. The servant suffered excruciating agony and before long was begging his master to shoot him. This is put on record as an instance of the painfulness of the phoorsa's bite, but to rub crystals of permanganate of potash into a skinned area of flesh could, in itself, have caused all the pain that was suffered. In fact, had the sufferer died I would have been inclined to attribute it to the permanganate rather than the snake. As it was the servant recovered, and was lucky not to have got gangrene.

The krait is another example of a poisonous but inoffensive snake. Its venom is deadly to a degree but it practically refuses to use it on a human being. Two boys once found a krait and captured it. Little knowing they were dealing with sudden death they then proceeded to tie it securely to a stick, a process which took some time. The snake, though trying desperately to escape, offered no retaliation and the boys proudly bore their captive home. The parents, who happened to know a krait when they saw one, did not share their sons' pride. The snake suffered death for its forbearance and the boys were well thrashed.

Amongst the Big Four the opposite to the conciliatory krait is the phoorsa mentioned above, also called the Saw-Scaled Viper. It is a small snake but that small body contains plenty of wickedness. It will bite savagely, and in captivity will try to strike at onlookers who are standing by its cage. Its bite, however, as I have said, is by no means always fatal.

In China, snakes are not popular, chiefly because they eat frogs, and the frog is almost a deity, being known as the Protector of the Rice. But frogs sometimes get their own back. They often eat very small snakes, and once, at a student's dissecting table, a 12-inch cobra was found inside a frog. Unfortunately it is not known whether the snake was taken alive or dead.

Frogs do remarkable things. In China a dog chased a 4½-inch rat into a bathroom. The rat ran down a pipe which let

117

out waste water into a tank outside. The observers dashed outside, hoping to kill the rat in the tank. All they found was a bull-frog with part of a rat's tail protruding from its mouth. It seemed in no distress, so the rat could not have been gnawing at its inside.

In Africa there are several species of cobra, including one that has the remarkable property of spitting poison through its teeth for a considerable distance, and with incredible accuracy. If the poison struck any part of an animal's body other than the eyes it would be harmless, so this snake aims for the eyes, and often scores a right and left. The result is agony for the recipient and sometimes permanent blindness. I had a pointer dog in Rhodesia that preceded me once into some bushes, suddenly gave a yelp of pain and came rushing out. It rubbed its head on the ground and continually passed its paws over its eyes. I got it home with great difficulty.

Although I had not seen the snake I knew what had happened and I knew what to do. The eyes must be bathed with a weak solution of potassium permanganate (the emphasis is on *weak*). Failing this, milk or even water is better than nothing.

It sounds simple; just as when a vet in England told me to put three drops of a medicine he made up into my spaniel's ears three times a day. Nothing could sound simpler, but actually nothing was more difficult. That spaniel fought like a wild cat when I tried to put the drops in. I doubt if in one week he got more than one drop into one ear, though his ear flaps were sodden with the mixture. The bottle finished I took him to the vet again, who said the treatment had brought great improvement, but I must continue it with another bottle. I asked if he would do it for a start, and explained the trouble I had had. He said there was no difficulty in putting drops into a dog's ear provided one was calm. I suggested it was the dog who ought to be calm, not I, and would he please calmly give the three drops into each ear whilst the dog was

118

there—which it was, waving its tail joyfully. The vet said he was busy, but if I'd leave the dog he'd have it done. This meant boarding fees, etc., so I departed with the bottle and a dog who evidently felt on top of the world—which was more than his master did. I think I am right in saying that *all* the drops from the new bottle missed the mark, but at the end of a week he was quite fit again.

Some people have difficult children, I have always had difficult dogs. All have fought violently against any treatment of any sort.

Perhaps it is I am not calm enough, so consider my position at this earlier time, faced with a dog (and a large one) frantic with pain and pawing at his eyes! A docile creature normally, he now tried to bite me whenever I tried even to look at his eyes. But bathe his eyes I was going to do, and did. It meant tying his feet and his mouth up and having a couple of natives to hold him down. In about two weeks he was all right. Actually the snake had only scored a bull on one eye.

One or two other snakes can spit poison and they are really the only snakes that use their poison at times for defence alone. True, the other snakes when they bite large animals are only defending themselves but they are doing so with a lethal weapon. A dose of poison from a spitting cobra, though it causes intense pain, never, unless injected, causes death.

Australia harbours a large number of snakes (over eighty species) of which the majority, to a greater or less degree, are poisonous. In this Australia is unique, for in all other countries where snakes abound the harmless ones far outnumber the venomous. These poisonous snakes do not possess anything like the amount of venom secreted by the notorious species of other parts of the world, though their venom is of unusually high toxicity.

All Australia's poisonous snakes are on the small side, the longest being about six feet, though a recently discovered species, *Oxyuranus maclennani* (The Giant Brown Snake) attains 10 feet.

Australia has no adders, in spite of the fact that one of the most venomous species is called the Death Adder. The reason is that it *looks* like an adder. It is not, however, an adder at all and injects a neurotoxic venom. It is never more than two feet long.

Rated among Australia's most dangerous snakes are the Death Adder, the Tiger Snake, the Black Snake and the Brown Snake.

The Tiger Snake, so called because of its striped colouring, is four to five feet long. It is quite a tiger, too, in the savagery of its attack. It has caused more fatalities than any other Australian snake.

The Black Snake is not really qualified to be classed as a dangerous species. Its venom has nothing like the toxicity of the Death Adder or the Tiger Snake.

The Brown Snake has a great reputation as a death-dealer though statistics do not altogether bear this out. Certainly its venom is highly toxic but the amount injected is small. It is a thin, graceful, inoffensive-looking snake of about five feet in length.

Ditmars, in his chapter 'Poisonous Snakes of Australia' gives the following statistics, compiled by Tidswell and Ferguson about these snakes:

The Death Adder. Of 10 persons bitten, 5 died.
The Tiger Snake.   Of 45 persons bitten, 18 died.
The Brown Snake. Of 70 persons bitten, 6 died.
The Black Snake.   Of 125 persons bitten, 1 died.

10

The Company of Vipers

Amongst the vipers we come across many famous names: the Rattlesnakes, the Fer de Lance, the Bushmaster, the Texas Diamond-Back (probably the most dangerous snake in the United States), the Copperhead, the Moccasins and others of America. Those occurring in Africa and Asia will be mentioned later.

Vipers are divided into two kinds, pit vipers and pitless vipers. Both kinds have the long front fangs which are kept in a sheath when not needed. The 'pit' is a small hole situated between the eye and the nostril, and until quite recently no one had any idea what its function was. I have mentioned before that snakes are unique in possessing certain gadgets and devices. Jacobson's organ is one, the organ that analyses the smells brought to it by the tongue, another is the egg-breaking machine in the gizzards of some snakes. But perhaps the most remarkable of them all is the pit of the pit vipers. It has now been found that the pit contains an extra sense found in no other animals. All animals of course can sense heat, but no other animal has a special organ so sensitive to heat that it can detect prey by the heat emanating from its body. A pit viper can detect the presence of a hidden rat or mouse by the quite negligible amount of heat given off at a distance.

121

The Company of Vipers

All the vipers in America are pit vipers. Africa has no pit vipers and Asia has both pit and pitless vipers.

In this book I am not describing the markings and colours of all the snakes I mention. For one reason I have read countless such descriptions and they have left me without the slightest idea of what the snake looked like, for it is almost impossible to describe a complicated pattern. For another the colouring of snakes is very variable. The only adequate thing is to have coloured plates of them all, including variations, which would push the price of the book up to the ceiling. When a snake is dead the colours soon fade, so museums are useful only for the markings. In reptile houses one rarely sees the snake one wants, it is either not there or has hidden itself in some nook. In any case, one can hardly expect a reader to drop the book and make a trip to a museum or reptile house whenever a snake is mentioned.

In America, or at any rate in the Wild West, to compare a man to a rattlesnake is to ask for serious trouble. It is almost as dangerous as calling him a horned toad—whatever a horned toad is. But the rattlesnake is no worse than a lot of other snakes. There are twenty-two species and of these only one or two are highly dangerous. All are poisonous to varying degrees, but several species are kept as pets and react well, often taking food from the fingers. Of course, many poisonous snakes are just as easy to keep as pets as non-poisonous ones, in fact easier, for quite a large number of non-poisonous snakes will bite without apparent provocation. A snake only bites either to kill prey or to defend itself, so once a poisonous snake knows its owner there is no reason for it to bite. But if any reader contemplates keeping a poisonous snake as a pet it must be remembered that all snakes are nervous; a door flung open, a careless wave of the hand, *may* induce a snake to strike.

Nevertheless there are several owners of rattlesnakes in America and so far as I know none of them has died of snake poison. And to keep *rattlesnakes* as pets increases the prestige

122

of the man who keeps them. According to one such man there is another advantage—if one is known as a rattlesnake owner one need never fear burglars. This is not borne out by the experiences of the Port Elizabeth Snake Park guardians, where, according to Fitzsimons, from time to time thieves break in at night to steal the snakes—to sell back again to the park.

The actual rattle of rattlesnakes is a series of horny cylindrical rings at the base of the tail. The baby rattlesnake comes into this world with a little button at the tip of its tail. In due course it sheds its skin, but a small portion cannot be shed owing to the button. This small portion dries into a cylinder, and as moults go on more horny cylinders are added, but not one for *every* moult, so one cannot tell the age of a rattlesnake by the number of hard cylinders as one can the age of a salmon by the rings on its scales. When the rattlesnake waves its tail, which it does when angry, these cylinders grate and knock together producing the famous rattle, which has been described as a sound like peas being shaken in a bladder.

Whether *all* abnormalities *must* have some use is, I think, questionable, but most people think they must, so the purpose of the rattle has caused much argument. The general idea was that the rattle was intended as a warning, but why should any snake warn its prey of its approach if it wants to capture it? It might, of course, be intended as a warning to large aggressors, but the rattlesnake's chief aggressors are those who *want* to find a rattlesnake; pigs and turkeys to kill and eat it, and deer who want to jump on it and kill it. Another suggestion is that the rattle halts, say, a rat or a mouse when it is running along. It stops and stands listening, and then the snake strikes. What it amounts to is that we can find no purpose for it. And why should we? There is a purpose for everything in a car or other piece of machinery, but not necessarily in an animal, even though an animal is much more intricate than a car.

The Company of Vipers

Rattlesnakes congregate in large numbers for hibernation, often travelling many miles to get to the rendezvous. The usual sort of place is a cave or cleft in a rock, and the rattlesnakes go there each year. A settler in the Rocky Mountains once built a home against a hill. It was winter and he was delighted with it. It was sheltered from cold winds and sun warmth reflected from the adjacent hillside made his place very cosy indeed. But spring came and one day hundreds of rattlesnakes appeared in his dwelling. They were emerging after hibernation, from a cleft adjoining the house. To have *one* rattlesnake in one's house must be sufficiently unnerving, but to have literally hundreds must be like something straight out of a tale by Edgar Allen Poe.

Nearly all the vipers produce living young, and these, like the young of all poisonous snakes, come into the world fully equipped with a poison apparatus. Being active and irresponsible they are considered to be more dangerous than their parents.

The Diamond Backed Rattler is the most dangerous. It packs a large dose of poison and is very ready to use it if it considers itself molested. It refuses food and dies if kept in captivity. The common Timber Rattlesnake is a docile creature and takes kindly to captivity, eating well and never biting. This is the snake that rattler enthusiasts keep as a pet and on that account are viewed with awe and admiration, for to most people a rattler is just a rattler whatever its species.

There is only one species of rattlesnake in South America. Amongst other names it is known as the Cascabel (*Crotalus durissus*). The Indians believe that a bite from this snake breaks the neck of its victim, and strange though this may sound, indirectly it may at times be true. The poison, unlike that of other rattlesnakes, contains a large amount of neurotoxin which seems to have a particularly powerful effect on the nerves and muscles of the neck. A bitten man has no control of his head, which lolls about as if his neck were broken. In this state, no doubt, the neck *could* easily be broken. It is also said that the victim, rolling about in his agony, does sometimes break his own neck. So far as I know, however, there are no recorded cases of this happening.

Before finishing with rattlesnakes I will, with apologies, relate a tall story about one of them that comes from America. A man was fishing by a river. The trout were rising freely but not one of them would have anything to do with his artificial fly. He decided to try natural bait and looked around for a frog. He could find none. Then he spotted a rattlesnake with a frog in its mouth. He tried to take the frog but the snake would not let it go. He had a flask of whisky in his hip pocket and poured some of this into the snake's mouth to make it release its hold. With this bait he caught a fine trout, and searched for another frog. He was still searching when he felt a nudge on his calf, and turned to find the rattlesnake with another frog in its mouth. Again he had to use whisky before the snake would release it. So it went on, the snake always appearing with a frog, until the fisher had a nice pile of trout. But the time came when the whisky was finished and the man got no more frogs and no more fish.

The Fer de Lance of tropical America is a venomous little creature, rarely exceeding six feet. It prefers to bite and ask questions afterwards. Like all snakes it is not actually aggressive, but it lies low and may be encountered unexpectedly when it bites at once.

One bite from a fer de lance once caused two deaths. A native woman used to make coconut sweets for sale. She grated the coconut herself on a nutmeg grater, so that the tips of her fingers were always more or less abrased. Her husband was a labourer, and one day he was brought home after being bitten by a fer de lance. He was taken to a native 'Snake Doctor' who got busy at once with whatever method it was he employed to cure snake bites. The wife had nothing to do except look on. Possibly to occupy her mind, the snake

125

doctor set her bathing the fang punctures, from which blood was still coming. The labourer died in two hours and his wife died the next morning, undoubtedly from poison absorbed through her finger-tips.

The Bushmaster is a large snake, second in length only to the King Cobra, but considerably stouter. Although the most notorious snake in South America it is not common, nor does it often bite, but it is venomous enough when it does.

'Snake Doctors' abound in tropical America. They treat snake bites with herbal remedies mixed with incantations and plenty of hocus pocus. It is fairly certain that, unlike, possibly, some African witch doctors, they possess no real cure but the natives often have more faith in them than in the recognized antivenine treatment. Curran and Kauffeld relate how, in the Panama Canal zone, a native was bitten by a bushmaster. The native was told to go to a certain clinic, and there everything was made ready to treat him immediately he arrived. He did not get there, nor did he arrive until two days later. He had been to a snake doctor in whom he had more faith than in the immaculate white-coated doctors at the clinic. I am sure that several things *are* cured by faith, but this was not one of them. When he arrived at the clinic he was in desperate plight, and although everything possible was done he died the next day.

Of the Moccasins the Water Moccasin is the best known and has been responsible for many deaths. In spite of this it is extremely docile and, in the opinion of some, makes the best pet of any of the snakes, poisonous or non-poisonous. A man who kept one used to take extraordinary liberties with it and merely laughed when told that he was being extremely rash. He even refused to believe that its bite was poisonous. One day a friend brought his dog along. The dog scented the snake and routed it out, to retire to a corner yelping the next second. It died in a few minutes. This so impressed the besotted owner that he presented his snake to the nearest zoo without delay.

The Company of Vipers

One of the most notorious of snakes is the Copperhead of North America. Its mere name is associated with sudden death in that continent. It is impossible to understand why, but people are so ready to believe ill of snakes that when one of them gets a bad name it sticks. It is one of the commonest snakes in the country and has certainly caused one or two deaths, but there is no getting round statistics. In 1928 and 1929, 308 persons were bitten by copperheads and none of them died, whether treated with antivenine or not.

The bad reputation of the copperhead is unfortunate for a harmless, very useful rat- and mouse-eating snake called the milk snake. There is some resemblance between the two. The resemblance is faint but any milk snake is nearly always killed for a copperhead and the killer congratulated all round as a benefactor to his fellows.

When Dr. Patrick Russell managed to get a certain snake named after himself in 1790 he achieved immortality, for the Russell Viper is one of the most famous of all snakes, and a member of the Big Four of India. I imagine Dr. Russell himself is already forgotten but his name lives on in the person of one of the most venomous of all the adders. Anyone desiring lasting fame should aim at inflicting his name on some animal or plant. It will confer more permanence than any title. Gentlemen in India seem to have been well aware of this and a list of snakes in that area of the globe reads rather like a telephone directory. Crowding on the heels of Russell come Wall, Mackinnon, Stoliczka, Beddome, Lunbrick, Jerdon, Thirston, Grey, Diard, Gunther, Blandford, Smith and enough others to fill several pages. Africa is far behind, very few snakes there having human names, and America, usually the headquarters of advertising, has acted with commendable restraint. But it does not matter what names they have; a rose, even if it is called Mrs. Henry Bodkins, smells just as sweet, and a snake is no more deadly for having a human name. They all have to be labelled and so long as we can recognize them and let the innocent ones go free no harm is done.

In India (as I have said before) Russell's Viper and the Phoorsa head the list of dangerous adders. The former is a stout and rather sluggish snake, but a beautiful one. Its ground colouring is buff marked with black spots and a delicate white tracery over the body that looks like fine lace. Its fangs are about half an inch long. A story about one of them may serve as a warning. A Mr. Slater of the geological department in India was described as being 'very fond' of snakes. One can be too 'fond' of snakes, especially if the subject is a Russell's viper. Anyway, one day Mr. Slater came across a Russell's viper asleep and put his foot on its neck to hold it down. This is one way *not* to pin down a snake. A boot is comparatively flat. The proper instrument is a forked stick. No doubt Mr. Slater thought himself safe because he was wearing leather leggings. With a boot the time comes when it has to be taken away, and that is the awkward moment. In this instance the snake twisted itself free of its own accord and immediately bit Mr. Slater *above* his leggings. He was able to get medical help fairly quickly and everything possible was done, but in spite of this he died in a few hours.

The Phoorsa is a small snake of about two feet. It is brown in colour (sometimes green), with a whitish line down each side of the back. It has small, white, triangular patches scattered along its length. When annoyed or surprised it bends itself about, its rough scales grating together and producing a sound like a piece of wood being sandpapered. It also inflates its lungs and hisses. It has the reputation of being very dangerous but it does not normally pack a really heavy punch. Lt.-Colonel Charpurey has estimated that only ten to twenty per cent of phoorsa bites are fatal.

The killing methods of these two adders are quite different. In a cage it was observed that the phoorsa (who likes to lie up in bushes) would wait in a bush until, say, a mouse passed underneath. Then its head would dart down and seize the mouse which would be firmly held until the poison took effect and its struggles ceased. The Russell's viper would lie coiled up in a corner and wait until something, such as a rat, came near. One quick strike would effect a bite and the viper would then appear to lose interest and go to sleep again. Later, it would go in search of the rat, which it knew must have died within a minute or so of being poisoned.

There are some forty other species of viper in Asia. All of them are labelled poisonous but the majority only inject poison of a strength sufficient to kill their small prey and which has little effect on a man. One or two, however, can inflict a fatal bite and others can give a bite that causes nausea, vomiting and fever that lasts for about twenty-four hours.

Africa possesses some six dangerous vipers, and in one of them has the distinction of possessing what is probably the most dangerous viper that lives—the Puff Adder. This is a large, heavy creature and though it rarely exceeds five feet its stoutness makes it appear one of the heavyweights. Usually, however, the specimens one meets in the veld are not more than about three feet.

The puff adder is a pretty snake with attractive markings of yellow, white and brown. Its dangerous-looking, wedge-shaped head is exceedingly broad at the base, as it has to be to contain the large poison glands. Its skin used to fetch a good price for the making of ladies' shoes and handbags. Since the colours fade after death these shoes and handbags were not to my mind particularly attractive, but at one time they were all the rage.

I was surprised when I read in a book by an American author that the puff adder is a drab, ugly snake. Evidently he had only seen stuffed specimens in a museum. A puff adder, especially when newly moulted, is a lovely thing. Another American went to the other extreme. He wrote that the puff **adder** and its close relatives are undoubtedly the most beautifully marked of all the snakes, which, I think, is questionable.

But handsome, they say, is as handsome does, and the puff adder does little that is handsome. When it bites, its fangs—those fearsome one-inch needles—penetrate deep down and the snake holds on, pumping in its venom. In some cases death has occurred in two minutes (probably owing to a vein being punctured) but anyone who receives a full dose of the poison has little hope, unless antivenine is quickly administered.

The same American writer who commented on the beauty of these vipers mentioned the extreme potency of the poison and went on to say that one might gather from this that they were exceedingly dangerous. This, he continued, is not so, 'the puff adder is too phlegmatic to be dangerous'.

It is precisely because of this that the puff adder *is* dangerous. Most snakes hear a man coming and when he arrives they are gone and he never even knows they were there. The lethargic puff adder finds a spot where the ground is warm, a native footpath or a patch in the grass, coils itself into a circle and goes to sleep. The next thing that may happen is that somebody treads on it and gets bitten immediately—for at such times the puff adder is not a bit phlegmatic. It is a case, of course, of a mistake on both sides, but it is too late for explanations.

A good mark for the puff adder is that it is inordinately fond of rats and mice, but this is not altogether a recommendation. Rats and mice abound chiefly in or near human habitations and attract the puff adders to these places, and with their proclivity for going to sleep at any odd time or in any spot they are not nice creatures to have around.

In other respects the puff adder is not aggressive. All it wants is a quiet life and a few rats.

As with most vipers the young are brought forth alive. They are active little creatures measuring about seven inches. Those who believe in the innocence of the very young must adjust that impression when it comes to puff adders. When newly born they already have fangs and poison glands and, like a child in possession of a hammer or a knife, they use their weapons with youthful irresponsibility. Fitzsimons found that a mouse bitten by a new-born puff adder died in two minutes and a rat in half an hour. A man bitten in the hand by a day-old youngster suffered from a swollen arm and constitutional disturbances for two or three days. The young waste no time in saying good-bye to mother, but scamper off to fend for themselves.

With toads and frogs puff adders rarely bother to use their poison but swallow them straight away. Fitzsimons once saw a large toad pursued by a puff adder. The puff adder caught it and swallowed it. Fitzsimons, interested, watched the swallowing process and then, after an interval, took his gun and blew the snake's head off. He cut the snake open, found the toad and took it out. It had been rolled into a sort of sausage which was covered with mucus. It showed no signs of life but after a lengthy period the sausage began to swell and faint movements could be seen. Still later, its limbs appeared and it sat up. Then it opened its eyes and looked around. Finally it waddled off into the bush, doubtless a very puzzled toad.

Most of us, I suppose, during our lives have had some escape from death that seems miraculous—as if Providence had directly interposed. I have had one and it so happens that my sister had one only a week ago (at the time of writing). I will relate my sister's experience first, though it has nothing to do with snakes. She stayed for a fortnight on a holiday at an hotel in Rottingdean. At meals she always had the same chair at the same table. The day of her departure came. She had invited a friend for lunch, her baggage was packed and the hotel staff tipped. She sat down at her usual chair at the usual table and her guest sat with her. Then the head waiter came up and said that there was a very nice table near the window. The usual occupants were away for lunch; would she go there? The table waiter came up and expostulated: he had put flowers specially on Miss Crompton's table. 'Then we will move them,' said the head waiter, and took the flowers to the other table. My sister and her guest moved there, and no sooner had they taken their seats than there was a terrific crash. A large and heavy chandelier had fallen right on to my sister's vacated chair, smashing the chair and part of the table.

My own experience seems (to me) just as miraculous if not so spectacular. I was on a patrol in Rhodesia, three weeks out. Food had run low and we (two native police, a boy and myself) had had no meat for a week. I left my tent one early morning and went out to see if I could shoot a buck. I walked very slowly and carefully so as not to make a sound, hoping to see some buck stealing through the grass. Then, on my left, behind a bush, I saw the horns of a reedbuck. My right foot was in mid air. The sight of the supposed buck made me draw that foot slowly back in order that I might retire a pace or two to get a better look. Immediately a loud hiss sounded from in front. I looked and saw a large puff adder coiled up with its head up in exactly the spot where my foot would have descended had I not withdrawn it. I had on only ankle boots with socks turned down and a pair of shorts. Had I not thought I saw this buck the adder would have got me in the bare calf. Antivenine was unknown. I did not even carry potassium permanganate crystals (not that they would have done any good) and it would have taken me a week to get to any outpost where a doctor could have been contacted.

It so turned out that there was no buck; the 'horns' were two branches behind the bush that bore a striking resemblance to a reedbuck's horns.

The Night Adder occurs all over South Africa. This is another snake that has gained a fearsome reputation with few qualifications. The common belief was that its bite was certain to be fatal. It *can* inflict a fatal bite on a man, but usually, after about two days' discomfort, the man is fit again.

The Company of Vipers

Even chickens, bitten in the thigh, have a chance of recovery, though if the worst should happen it takes about a day to kill them. Moreover, it is exceedingly difficult to make a night adder bite at all. A farmer once put his hand down a hole and unknowingly pulled out a night adder. The snake made no attempt to bite but fled the instant it was released.

Fitzsimons tells of a farmer who was bitten in the thumb by a night adder. It was about midday and believing that night adders were amongst the most deadly of snakes the farmer sat for hours in a chair, sucking his thumb. If he had not done this he might have been alive today. The hours went by and he felt no symptoms from the bite, but later his throat began to swell. The swelling got worse and finally he died purely from suffocation at about seven p.m. The reason seems fairly clear. He must have had a 'sore' throat which was a little raw, or, perhaps, ulcerated gums. The bite in the thumb had obviously done him practically no harm in itself but the poison sucked into the mouth was deadly. The membranes of the mouth and throat are exceedingly sensitive. The poison acted on the raw surfaces and caused swelling which finally blocked the air passage. Had a tube been inserted in the windpipe the farmer would have been all right, for the swelling would have subsided in due course.

Actually, provided there are no abrasions in the mouth, sucking a snake bite wound immediately (and spitting out) is one of the best ways of getting rid of what poison has not already been absorbed. The mouth, however, should always be first rinsed with a solution of potassium permanganate and the rinsing continued at intervals just in case there may be any sore place.

Those who have kept them say night adders make wonderful pets; lively, never refusing food and perfectly safe to handle. It is one of the few adders that lays eggs.

The Berg Adder is found in mountainous regions in South Africa. It is infinitely more venomous than the night adder. In captivity it refuses food and dies.

The Company of Vipers

The Gaboon Viper of North Africa is as large as its relative the puff adder, and just as venomous, though not so common. It has been classed by some as being the most beautiful of all snakes. Never having seen one alive I cannot say. An American naturalist writes, 'A carpet made in the pattern of the Gaboon viper would call forth the admiration and envy of everyone, so beautifully is this creature marked.'

There are two horned adders. The 'horns' are erect scales. One, *Bitis caudalis*, has one horn over the eyes, the other, *Bitis cornuta*, has two, one over each eye. They are about two feet long and the latter is known as the Asp, made famous by being chosen by Cleopatra as her executioner. And if Cleopatra encouraged it to pump all its poison into her it might well have killed her, though it is not a particularly venomous reptile. It lives in sandy deserts and has the habit, the reverse of the ostrich, of burying its body and leaving its head exposed, to the discomfort of any lizard, or bare-footed man, that passes by.

Britain makes a very poor showing in respect of snakes. There are three species in England, the Grass Snake, the Smooth Snake and the Adder. The first two are non-venomous and are only found in England. The smooth snake is very rare and the grass snake, thanks to the way this pretty and useful creature is almost always killed on sight, is disappearing. The adder is fairly plentiful and is found both in England and Scotland. Ireland, of course, like New Zealand, possesses no snakes.

Since there are so many species of adders in the world, to call the British adder The Adder seems rather strange, but since Britain possesses only one adder the popular name is descriptive enough, and one can hardly expect ordinary people to go about calling it *Vipera berus berus*. I am all for popular names, when such exist, but there are many who are not. I once went with some members of a natural history society to which I belong on a fungus hunt. After some

134

The Company of Vipers

search I went up to the leader and said, 'I've got a Death Cap and a Fly Agaric.' He said, 'Oh, an *Amanita phalloides* and an *Amanita muscaria*—I never use those popular names.' Crushed, I went off to search for some more, hoping I would know their scientific names, but doubting it.

The adder has a broad, brown zigzag stripe down its back. The stripes of the males are darker than those of the females. Variations occur occasionally and there have been cases of adders without the zigzag lines. But there was no excuse for a caller, an amateur naturalist, who visited me recently proudly carrying the body of a grass snake and saying he had killed an adder. He had had a lot of trouble but, by manœuvring, had managed to run his car over it. The markings were the typical markings of the grass, or ring, snake, white 'dog-collar' and all. Had he been in Scotland the caller would have been on safe ground, for there every snake is an adder.

The adder is a hardy little beast. Unlike the bulk of snakes it does not insist on a warm climate. It even lives in Scandinavia and Finland. In Britain, after hibernating, it has often been seen, if the sun is shining, lying in the snow and sunning itself. If disturbed it will burrow in snow.

Adders are often kept in captivity though they do not make very good pets. They will eat and can be handled, and when handled do not strike. But they do not like being handled. If caught when elderly, adders are very difficult to tame at all. These, said a writer on the subject, should be let go. I smiled to myself when I thought of the reactions of the neighbours if they knew that someone was releasing elderly adders.

Like almost every slightly venomous snake, the adder has got itself a fearful reputation. Since in this country we have only one venomous snake this is not surprising; we have to make the most of it.

Actually, the adder's poison is deadly enough for its small prey; shrews, lizards, etc., but so is the venom of a spider for a fly. It does not follow that it has the same effect on a man. Let us look at what records there are. For fifty years, up to

The Company of Vipers

1945, there were only seven fatal cases of adder bites, four of them children. That is very few. In such a long period bees and wasps could claim far more victims (my own son was nearly killed by a bee sting and was only saved by the doctor arriving in time). And so could gnats. With predisposed, unhealthy people, young or old, any bite, or even a scratch from a blackthorn, can set up poisoning with fatal results. In the case of the adder the disturbances are intensified because the victim suffers from shock, always thinking an adder bite is fatal. If bee or wasp stings were thought to be fatal, what mortality there would be from them! As it is, a man stung by either merely mutters an impolite word, suffers the pain and swelling and gets on with his work, after (or not) daubing the puncture with his favourite remedy, from onions to blue-bags. More impressive than a list of deaths would be a list of those bitten by adders who recovered—but such cases rarely come to light; they are not 'news'.

I lived for several years near Dartmoor and in a local pub met a labourer. He told me he had once been bitten in the hand by an adder. He said there was swelling and he felt pain, but he went back to work next morning with a diminished swelling that gave no pain, but itched.

I also talked to a cook-housekeeper whose boy of five had also been bitten in the hand. She said there was swelling that extended right up to the elbow, and the child was irritable and sometimes whimpered. She gave no treatment, not knowing what to do, and in two days the child was back at school with next to no symptoms but a slight discoloration at the seat of the bite.

Now comes the sad story of a child bitten by an adder, again in the hand, whose parents pursued the proper course. This occurred in 1959 and was reported in the newspapers. There was only local swelling and no general symptoms. He was whisked off to a doctor and antivenine was injected. The boy died shortly afterwards, *not* from the bite of the adder but from the antivenine to which he was evidently violently

The Company of Vipers

allergic. This, of course, could only happen in the case of about one in a thousand. It is ironic that it was bad luck for the child to have had such conscientious parents.

A week ago, as I write, I was holding forth to some visitors and saying that I considered the adder's bite normally little more dangerous than the sting of a bee. The next day the newspapers gave prominence to a girl who had been bitten by an adder and had died. This, said my wife, made me look pretty silly, and I expect the visitors thought so too. But the day following the papers reported that four more children had been bitten by adders, including a child only a few months old. They had been rushed off (one by air) for treatment and all had recovered. The journeys had taken some time but I could find no mention of any alarming symptoms. And in the same papers was the report of a man of fifty-three who had died from the sting of a bee. It was stated that the doctors thought the girl who had died had had the poison injected direct into a vein. This would aggravate matters but would hardly have caused death in a normal person.

Everyone has heard of the 'Dance of the Adders' and it was always supposed to be a courting display. Two adders face each other in a semi-erect position, swaying about. They sway backwards and forwards and sideways, and often touch and press on each other and make many elaborate movements. Naturally, they were thought to be male and female but it is now known that they are always two males and that, far from courting, they are fighting—each trying to claim territory. Very sensibly, they never bite each other and finally one of them drops down and streaks off. We have no clue as to the rules of these contests or what makes one of them decide he is the loser. Anyway, it is all very clean.

11

Serpents in the Sea

─────◦∿∿∪∿∿◉∿∿∿∿◦─────

Like many reptiles (and mammals) some snakes returned to the water whence all of them had originally come. But, unlike the other reptiles, and the mammals, no fundamental changes such as occurred with the whale had to come about. Whilst on land, snakes had completely altered their shapes and method of progression to make them better fitted for their land lives but it so happened, and it was a complete fluke, that this changed shape not only made them better adapted for the land but for the water also.

So some took permanently to the water. They did not need much pursuading; all snakes love water and all snakes can swim with grace and speed, though not all of them get the chance. Some of these reversionists took to freshwater and some to the sea. They did undergo a very slight modification in doing this; the nostrils came to lie on top of the snout instead of at the sides, and, with many, the nostrils could be closed so that the snake could stay for hours under water. Freshwater snakes are usually called simply 'water snakes' and the others 'sea snakes'.

Even land snakes are very tolerant of submersion. An anatomist, having no chloroform and wishing to kill a krait, put one in a cigar box and submerged it in water. He left it submerged for two hours but when he took the box out he found the snake unharmed.

Serpents in the Sea

There are many species of water snakes in the world and North America contributes the largest number. They frequent lakes, pools and rivers, swimming like eels and catching fish. Indeed, keen fishermen who pay large sums for the privilege of fishing in preserved waters have become alarmed at the number of fish water snakes are supposed to consume. It has been pointed out that a water snake is no match in speed with a trout and so is unlikely to take any, but a trout cannot see backwards and often lies motionless facing the current. At these times it would be an easy prey for a stealthy water snake coming up from behind. And water snakes must work havoc with fish fry, for they are voracious feeders.

But there is nothing the fishing people can do about it—at any rate, not much. The water snake is one of the most difficult of all creatures to locate, let alone kill. If swimming on the surface with only its nostrils exposed, it dives like a dabchick on any disturbance to reappear (or not) a long distance away. It hides under stones, in crevices in rocks or tree trunks, or lies submerged in mud in the reeds.

It is commonly stated that water snakes are non-poisonous. This is mostly true but there are exceptions, such as the freshwater cobra of Africa. Harmless though most of them are, nearly all of them are 'vicious' and bite savagely at the slightest provocation. In captivity most of them lose this viciousness and can be handled freely. A lot of species can be kept in an ordinary cage with merely a bowl of water in the corner. They are, as I have said, voracious and when their owner comes with a piece of fish the odour of it reaches them long before they get it and they become as excited as a kennelful of pups, dashing about and even biting each other.

Other species will not eat dead fish. They are usually kept in a tank with the bough of some tree protruding above. Water snakes, though clumsy on land, like to climb into bushes or trees that overhang water. There they wait sunning themselves until they see some fish just below, when they drop down and try to capture it. In captivity they lie on the

139

bough and at feeding time live fish are put into the tank. They dive in and pursue the fish with open mouths. In a few minutes there are no more fish. There are some species of water snakes who in captivity remain dour and sullen and continue to bite the hand of the man who tries to feed them. They refuse all food and die.

There is a peculiar river snake in Indo-China called *Herpeton tentaculatum* which has two appendages above its nostrils that look like worms. These are kept in perpetual motion, wriggling about. They act as bait, for fishes often rush at them and are caught.

None of the water snakes are particularly good looking. They range from about two feet to five feet in length and some are stout and heavy. They do not insist on the water being fresh but will live in brackish lakes and in the upper reaches of estuaries. It has been fairly well established that they will have no dealings with warm-blooded animals, rats, mice or birds, but confine themselves to fish, frogs, toads, tadpoles and the like.

While certain snakes took to rivers and lakes, others took to the sea. These were of the cobra tribe and there were no half measures in their action; into the sea they went and in the sea they have remained, so that today most of them, if stranded on the shore, are as helpless as fishes. As adaptations they have acquired large lungs and self-closing nostrils on the top of the head. Although they have no gills it has been suggested that they may be able to use the oxygen in the water. They also possess flattened, paddle-like tails which can drive them through the water at speed. They have completely relinquished their association with land. They are air-breathing creatures but can remain under water for many hours, swimming about and chasing fish.

Their success has been tremendous. They inhabit the sea in vast numbers and there are fifty-five species. On the whole they confine themselves to the warmer belts.

Serpents in the Sea

The bulk of them bring forth their young alive, selecting quiet pools near the shore for the purpose. Some, however, lay eggs, and these, at the right time, wriggle a short distance on to the land to do so.

Sea snakes pair in the spring. In the Persian Gulf a ship's officer saw two of them in the water, locked together. He and another went off in a boat and fished them up with a boat-hook. They were then taken to the ship and put on the deck. Neither of them took any notice of this rough handling, nor desisted from their occupation. In general, copulation, with snakes, lasts from an hour to a whole day and is often indulged in day after day.

In contra-distinction to the freshwater snakes who are non-venomous but vicious, all the sea snakes are highly venomous but very unaggressive. Native fishermen off Ceylon and India frequently bring up numbers of them in their nets and treat them with contempt, seizing them anywhere and throwing them back. Colonel Charpurey and several American writers say that there is no record of anyone having been bitten by a sea snake, but Fitzsimons states of African species, 'Many fatalities have occurred by people mistaking them for eels and catching hold of them,' and goes on to describe how a naval officer and, on another occasion, a naval rating took hold of one, were bitten and died in an hour or so.

One would have thought that there must have been *some* unrecorded casualties amongst the native fishers who treat sea snakes with such contempt. On the other hand there cannot have been many, for news spreads and one accident would result in the natives treating these snakes with more respect. They are scared enough of land snakes, both the poisonous and non-poisonous varieties.

Their forbearance is well illustrated by the experience of a man who decided to swim from his ship to the shore. The ship was anchored off the Pacific side of the Panama Canal. Half-way to land he found to his horror that he was swimming in the midst of thousands of snakes. They passed him in shoals, practically touching him. When they reached the shore he had, perforce, to land with them. None of them offered him the slightest harm, nor even took any notice of him.

These snakes being descended from cobras, have poison that is neurotoxic and experiments have proved it deadly to mammals. It is even more deadly to cold-blooded creatures, and any fish a sea snake bites is killed almost immediately. The prey, of course, is always swallowed head first so that the fins do not impede the process.

For some unknown reason sea snakes do not exist in the Atlantic, though they abound in the Pacific Ocean. It was thought that when the Panama Canal was cut sea snakes would get through it into the Atlantic. So far this has not happened, possibly because there is a freshwater lake in the middle of the route, called Gatun Lake, which they would have to go through. Sea snakes, however, can go considerable distances up tidal rivers and into water that has but little salt.

So, serpent being synonymous with snake, there *are* sea serpents. But the largest is only about ten feet long, which does not at all fit in with the usual conception. There has for long been an eager demand for a sea serpent of the right dimensions, and from time to time astute people have done their best to satisfy it. Several American newspaper editors and reporters have invented enormous monsters in various places and printed the accounts of observers, who were about as genuine as the monster. But it gave a fillip to the sales of the paper. Even alleged scientists have not been guiltless. In America one such collected the fossil bones of mastodons and similar huge creatures and with ingenuity worthy of a better cause fixed these bones together to form a skeleton purported to be that of a huge sea serpent. In the same country a struggling journalist who wished to call attention to himself made a large inflatable sea serpent out of rubber and attached it to a wire that ran under water across a narrow estuary near his

142

house. When the wire was slackened the inflated serpent appeared above the water, and the swell rolled it about in a life-like way. When this journalist had visitors (which he soon did in plenty) he made the serpent appear for a few minutes, then someone tautened the wire and drew it under.

Yet I suppose there was *some* reason for the myth of the sea serpent. Our foreparents believed in it implicitly. Several witnesses genuinely believed they had seen one. Amongst these was a Royal Navy Commander, who noted it in his log. Several explanations have been given. Curran and Kauffeld give what is perhaps the most likely. They believe the monsters seen were giant squids. These monsters, thirty and more feet long and very broad, live in the depths of the sea. They are preyed on by the sperm whale, but occasionally the whales encounter specimens too large for them to cope with. In the struggle the squid may then be brought to the surface where its body in the lesser pressure becomes so filled with gas that it is unable to return below. It would then travel on the surface and, since it always goes backwards, its hind end, which looks like the head of a huge rocket, would be above the surface. The rest of it beneath the water would naturally be assumed by any onlooker to be a hundred or more feet long. From that it only needed a little imagination for sailors to describe sea serpents throwing their coils round a fully rigged sailing vessel and drawing it under, after first swallowing the men on deck.

Mankind loves monsters and is always ready to believe in them. (The Loch Ness monster and the Abominable Snowman are present-day examples.) Perhaps in the remote future he may get a real sea serpent of the proper dimensions. In the sea there seems no limit to the size that animals can attain by evolution. The mighty whale is supposed to have originated from a land mammal about the size of a small dog. Therefore there is nothing to prevent one of our sea snakes in time acquiring the length and girth that so far sea serpents have only possessed in fables.

12

Snake Hunters

———•∿∿∿∿∿◉∿∿∿∿∿•———

On television recently an interviewer spoke to a 'snake hunter' in Australia. This man said he went out and caught snakes by the tail and killed them. The two then went out to try and find a snake and demonstrate. Everyone who has tried to do this knows how difficult it is to find a snake when you want one. It generally takes about a month or longer. Strangely enough, these two found one straight away in a field close by, and strangely enough, it made no attempt to streak off to safety. The snake was picked up by the tail and, equally strangely, did not flash back at the hand. Once a snake is held aloft by its tail it is helpless, provided it is swung to and fro so that it cannot coil up round itself and reach the hand that holds it, but it is a very different matter when the tail is on the ground and I advise no one to try it—unless the snake has been specially treated beforehand. The 'snake hunter' swung the snake round in circles and then bashed its head against the ground. The interviewer turned round to the camera with a broad, proud grin on his face.

Now we saw another very remarkable coincidence. There were several other snakes within a few feet of the place where the first had been found, and none of them had made any attempt at a getaway. Nor did they now. All of them were bashed to death, and the pleased, fatuous smile of the interviewer increased with each death. Evidently he quite thought his audience were going to share his delight. I only know two

144

of them, my daughter was one and she had long since fled the room; I remained, determined to see this butchery to an end but very frustrated at not being able to wipe out that grin from the interviewer's face.

After the slaughter a few questions were asked. One of them was, in what time would a bite from one of these snakes cause death? (Incidentally, the species of the snake was not mentioned.) The answer was, quarter of an hour. Now, those who have any knowledge at all about snakes know that it is impossible to tell what time a bite from any snake takes to kill a man. It may be minutes, hours or days; or he may not die at all.

Evidently the producers of this particular programme thought that all humanity so detested snakes that they would take pleasure in seeing them suffering crude execution. I grant the hatred but not the rest. Mad dogs are a thousand times more dangerous than snakes but I doubt if an audience would like to see them having their heads bashed on the ground.

I admit that really poisonous snakes should be killed when met with, but more in sorrow than in anger. We are so lamentably incompetent at killing our chief enemies, rats and mice, that we might spare some gratitude for those who do it so much better than we do. Personally, I do not understand why we do not import snakes. The House, Rat and Mole snakes of South Africa are completely harmless to man and do no damage to him or his crops or his lifestock (except perhaps a few chickens), but they do a tremendous amount of damage to rats and mice. Whether they would survive our winters I do not know but I do not see why not; the southern parts of Africa are bitterly cold in winter, and they survive there.

Ireland might also consider the idea. The inhabitants brag about having no snakes, but I know from experience they have plenty of rats.

But so long as men continue to think that in killing any snake at all they are on a par with Saint George slaying a dragon, such importations are unlikely.

145

Bibliography

Amongst the books consulted were the following:

Bell, T. (1839). *A History of British Reptiles*. London: John Van Voorst.

Bellairs, Angus d'A. (1957). *Reptiles*. London: Hutchinson's University Library. New York: Rinehart and Coy.

Boulenger, E. G. (1914). *Reptiles and Batrachians*. London: Dent.

Boulenger, G. A. (1913). *The Snakes of Europe*. London: Methuen.

Charpurey, Lieut.-Col. K. G. (1954). *The Snakes of India and Pakistan*. Bombay: The Popular Book Depot. London: Luzac and Coy, Ltd. New York: Wm. S. Heinman.

Cochran, D. M. (1943). *Poisonous Reptiles of the World*. Washington: Smithsonian Institute.

Curran, C. H. and Kauffeld, C. (1937). *Snakes and their Ways*. New York: Harper.

Ditmars, R. L. (1936). *Reptiles of the World*. New York: Macmillan.

Ditmars, R. L. (1946). *Snakes of the World*. New York: Macmillan.

Fitzsimons, F. W. (1912). *The Snakes of South Africa*. Cape Town: T. Maskew Miller.

Fitzsimons, F. W. (1932). *Snakes*. London: Hutchinson.

Hopley, C. C. (1882). *Snakes*. London: Griffith and Farran.
146

Bibliography

Leighton, G. R. (1901). *The Life History of British Serpents.* Edinburgh: Blackwood.

Loveridge, A. (1946). *Reptiles of the Pacific World.* New York and London: Macmillan.

Matthews, L. H. (1952). *The British Amphibia and Reptiles.* London: Methuen.

Pope, C. H. (1956). *The Reptile World.* London: Routledge and Kegan Paul.

Smith, Malcolm. (1951). *The British Amphibians and Reptiles.* London: Collins.

Wall, F. (1908). *The Poisonous Terrestrial Snakes of our British India Dominions.* Bombay: Natural History Society.

Wall, F. (1921). *Snakes of Ceylon.* Colombo: H. R. Cottle, Gov. Printer, Ceylon.

Williston, S. W. (1914). *Water Reptiles of the Past and Present.* Chicago: The University of Chicago Press.

I am also indebted to the journals of the Bombay Natural History Society from which I have gained much information.

147

Index

Index

Curran, C. H., and Kauffeld, C., 41, 104, 126, 143

Dasypeltis scaber, 37
Death adder, 120
Decomposition, 75
Dendraspis viridis, 72
Diamond-backed rattlesnake, 124
Digestion, 31
Dogs, as snake killers, 51, 52; and pythons, 96, 97; and black mamba, 105, 106; and water moccasin, 126
Dormouse, hibernation of, 61, 62
Drymarchon corais couperi, 41

Ears, 20, 21
Earth snake, 92
Eggs: and snakes, 36–8; of python, 99
Eizenberger, Dr., 72
Enemies, 47–57
Eyes, 15, 16

Fasting, of snakes, 99
Fayrer, Dr., 76, 87, 88
Fer de Lance, 121, 125, 126
Fitzsimons, F. W., 75, 82–4, 93, 104, 105, 141
Food, of snakes, 30–40
Footballer, killed by mamba, 106, 107
Frogs, 29, 31, 56, 64, 117

Gaboon viper, 134
Grass snake, 22, 41, 42, 134
Green mamba, 72

Hamadryad (see Cobra, King)
Herpeton tentaculatum, 140
Hibernation, 58–68; of mammals, 60; of dormice, 62; of

hedgehogs, 62; of bats, 62; of badgers, 63; of bears, 63; of snakes and reptiles, 63; of snakes, 67, 68; of rattlesnakes, 124
House snake, 30, 32, 46, 145
Hunter, John, 67

Immunity from snake poison, 47
Indigo snake, 41

Killing, art of, 101
King cobra (see Cobra, King)
Krait, 116, 117, 138

Lung fish, 65
Lungs, 18

Mamba, 14, 21, 42, 48, 69, 70, 103–110; green, 72; toxicity of poison, 105; and dogs, 105, 106; causes death of footballer, 106, 107; experience with, 109, 110
Meercat, 51
Mesmerism, 39
Mice, 23
Milk snake, 127
Milking by snakes, 40
Moccasin, 121; and dog, 126; water, 126
Mole snake, 30, 43, 145
Mongoose, 47, 48
Monitor, 96
Monkeys, and snakes, 39, 40
Movement of snakes, 13

Native snake bite cures, 80
Night adder, 132, 133

Pet snakes, 41–6
Pigs, 47; as snake killers, 56

149

Index